MARTIN BJERGEGAARD is a serial entrepreneur and an international bestselling author. He is the co-founder of Rainmaking, Startupbootcamp, Frokost.dk and BetterNow .org and, most recently, Rainmaking Loft. His bestselling book, *Winning Without Losing*, has been translated into fifteen languages and won the prestigious Management Book of the Year award from the Chartered Management Institute and the British Library. Martin is also the author of *The Great Idea*, an entrepreneurial fairy tale for children.

COSMINA POPA is an entrepreneur whose experience is firmly rooted in the technology and sustainability sectors. In 2013, she, together with a team based in Washington DC, co-founded the Conscious Venture Lab, a start-up accelerator focussed on developing socially conscious entrepreneurs. She holds an MSc in Environment and International Development from King's College London, and a BA in Liberal Arts from St John's College, Maryland, USA.

Also by Martin Bjergegaard

Winning Without Losing

The Great Idea

HOW TO BE A LEADER

Martin Bjergegaard
and Cosmina Popa

PICADOR

New York

www.picadorusa.com • picadorbookroom.tumblr.com
www.twitter.com/picadorusa • www.facebook.com/picadorusa

Picador® is a U.S. registered trademark and is used by St. Martin's Press under license from Pan Books Limited.

For book club information, please visit www.facebook.com/ picadorbookclub or e-mail marketing@picadorusa.com.

Designed by Steven Seighman

The photographic credits on pages 211 and 212 constitute an extension of this copyright page.

The Library of Congress Cataloging-in-Publication Data is available upon request.

ISBN 978-1-250-07873-5 (trade paperback)
ISBN 978-1-250-07874-2 (e-book)

Picador books may be purchased for educational, business, or promotional use. For information on bulk purchases, please contact Macmillan Corporate and Premium Sales Department at 1-800-221-7945, extension 5442, or write specialmarkets@macmillan.com.

Originally published in Great Britain by Macmillan, an imprint of Pan Macmillan, a division of Macmillan Publishers Limited.

First U.S. Edition: August 2016

10 9 8 7 6 5 4 3 2 1

Contents

Introduction

1. Bystanders vs leaders

The murder of Kitty Genovese on 13 March 1964 has influenced Western psychology, culture and consciousness more than anyone thought possible. Besides making nationwide headlines at the time, it sparked a whole new field of scientific research for decades to follow, it has been studied in several bestselling books (including two from 2014), and it has served as inspiration for numerous songs, movies and theatre plays. The misdeed also accelerated the implementation of the 911 emergency system, which became a reality across the United States in 1968.

What was so special about this crime? With 636 murders in New York City during the year of 1964, another spilled life was sad, but hardly much of a public affair. Yes, the murder was brutal, and the victim was a pretty young woman, but that alone was far from outstanding. Kitty wasn't famous and she didn't have friends in high places. So it was no surprise that for the first ten days the incident didn't get much attention at all. But then something happened.

A. M. Rosenthal was relatively new on the job as the metropolitan editor of the *New York Times*. He was very ambitious, and he often had lunch meetings with New York City's police commissioner, Michael Murphy, to scout for particularly juicy crimes to report on. During one of their lunch meetings Murphy shared how it surprised him that this twenty-eight-year-old bar manager, Kitty Genovese, had been chased, stabbed, sexually assaulted, and eventually killed, in the middle of the street, and yet no one had even bothered to call the police.

It wasn't that Kitty didn't scream. She did. A lot. During the investigation the police had to interview thirty-eight eyewitnesses, all of whom had either seen or heard Kitty sometime during the almost thirty minutes it took the twenty-nine-year-old Winston Moseley to commit his random act of cruelty. Moseley was on his own, unknown in the neighbourhood, and the only weapon he brought on the day was a hunting knife. So why did no one come to Kitty's rescue, or at least make an effort to alert the police?

Rosenthal went away from that lunch feeling that he was on to something big. Three days later the *New York Times* ran a front-page story with a four-column headline:

> 37 WHO SAW MURDER
> DIDN'T CALL THE POLICE
> Apathy at Stabbing of Queens
> Woman Shocks Inspector

The article opened with:

> For more than half an hour 38 respectable, law-abiding citizens in Queens watched a killer stalk and stab a woman in three separate attacks in Kew Gardens.

Readers were seemingly forgiving of the minor inconsistency on the number of witnesses, and soon the story was on everyone's lips. As the police report came out, two quotes from the passive bystanders won particular fame. A neighbour and friend of Kitty's had opened his front door, been face to face with the killer for a moment, only to quickly close the door again. To the police he explained, 'I didn't want to get involved.' In another apartment a woman had said to her husband, 'Thirty people must have called the police by now.'

Millions of Americans were outraged, as well as moved to tears, and it was widely debated how something like this could have happened. Possible explanations ranged from numbness caused by growing television consumption to the cynicism appearing in big cities, with some simply dismissing the human race as selfish, fearful and lacking any real sense of empathy.

Modern-day reviews of the case have shown that Rosenthal had got a bit carried away and exaggerated some of the facts he learnt during these three days in 1964, reading police reports, studying witness statements and talking to neighbours. There was actually one person who shouted out the window 'Leave that girl alone', which prompted Moseley to stop his attack and return to his car. But only to come back. There was also an old woman who came out after the murderer had left, and she was holding the dying Kitty Genovese in her arms when the police finally arrived. One person claims that he did call the police, but was ignored. And the scared neighbour who had slammed the door because he 'didn't want to get involved', in his panic

took the back door to a friend in the same building. After long discussions (and when it was too late
to save Kitty) he did in fact muster up the courage
to give the police a ring. Finally, there had been two
attacks on Genovese, not three, and the latter of
them had taken place out of sight of the eyewitnesses.

Despite these exaggerations, the murder of Kitty
Genovese gave food for thought. It touched on a
deep and primal fear: 'If my life should be in dan-
ger, would anyone come to help me?' Moseley
quickly went behind bars (where he still is), but this
kind of fear has more to do with our human nature
than with any one psychopath. The incident made
us question ourselves. Answers were needed.

Social psychologists Bibb Latané, John Darley
and Judith Rodin were the first to provide the public with a scientifically solid explanation. Following the 1964 ordeal they promptly went on to
conduct a series of experiments. One of their studies, published in 1969, revealed that whilst 70 per
cent would help a woman in distress when they
were the only witness, only about 40 per cent took
action when other people were also present.

In another experiment, participants were brought
in supposedly to fill out questionnaires. Some were
placed in a room alone, whilst others were seated

together with two other people, either fellow participants or researchers posing as participants. As they sat filling out questionnaires, smoke began to fill the room. When participants were alone, 75 per cent reported the smoke to the experimenters. By contrast, just 38 per cent of participants in a room with two other participants reported the smoke. In the final group, when the participants were paired with two researchers in disguise, who noted but ignored the smoke, only 10 per cent of the participants reported it.[1]

This phenomenon became known as *bystander apathy* or the *bystander effect*, and it went a long way to explaining why there had been no help for Kitty Genovese that night in Kew Gardens. Simply put, the more people who *can* help, the fewer actually *will* help. This is attributed to two psychological principles. The first is *diffusion of responsibility*: 'With this many people around, why should *I* help?' Action or inaction becomes a shared responsibility. The group makes a decision, not the individual. Unfortunately, group decision-making is a dreadful mechanism in emergency situations.

The second principle is that of *social influence*, which means that, when something unexpected happens, bystanders will monitor the reactions of other people as their main input as to whether action is necessary. A bunch of passive bystanders provide *social proof* to each other that it's okay not to step up and help.

Now that we've seen an example of bystander apathy, let's look at a case which tells a different story. A story of one leader emerging from the crowd of bystanders.

Due to a fatal combination of a heavy snowstorm and a range of serious pilot errors, Air Florida Flight 90 only managed to climb 107 metres before starting to decline on 13 January 1982. Within thirty seconds of take-off, and just two miles from the White House, the plane struck the 14th Street Bridge, plunged through the ice and sank immediately in the Potomac River. On board were seventy-four terrified passengers and five crew members.

Only six people made it out of the plane wreckage and surfaced amidst twisted metal and broken ice. Injured, shocked and trapped in below-zero-degree water, the survivors needed help to come ashore. Unfortunately, the bad weather had caused traffic jams all over the city, and the emergency vehicles struggled to get to the site. However, the lines of cars stuck in traffic meant that plenty of people had seen the startling accident, and after a few minutes close to a hundred people had arrived, including emergency personnel. But no one had any ideas as to how to get to the survivors, and the situation was becoming desperate. The crowd watched as the six survivors kept fighting for their lives, holding on to floating metal parts and ice flakes, screaming and begging for help.

At 4.20 p.m., nineteen minutes after the crash, a rescue helicopter finally arrived. With the bridge so close, and all the fragments in the water, this was a difficult mission. The helicopter crew lowered a lifebuoy to the first survivor to tow him to shore. It took time to get him through the icy water safely, but the effort was successful.

On the second trip one of the survivors managed to hold on to two of the other survivors who by now were too weak to make it on their own. Unfortunately, during the tow one of them, Priscilla Tirado, fell off. Blinded by jet fuel, panicked, and being pushed beneath the surface by the wind pressure from the helicopter that was trying to save her, things looked very dire for Priscilla.

Now close enough to shore for the bystanders to look into her wide-open, blinded eyes, her plight is a heart-breaking sight to behold. With journalists and cameramen in the bystander crowd, all that happened was documented and is readily available on YouTube. It's easy to be moved to tears whilst watching Priscilla up close, as she is making her last desperate moves, and it's obvious that within seconds she will be gone.

Unable to hold on to the lifebuoy, she cannot be saved. Or so it seems. The bystanders are holding their breath, many are crying. The whole thing seems to be happening in slow motion, with Priscilla's movements stiff and awkward in her severe state of hypothermia.

Then suddenly one of the bystanders moves forward, rips off his boots and coat, and with determination throws himself into the water. With clumsy but efficient strokes Lenny Skutnik swims towards Priscilla. He arrives, pulls her head above water, tows her with his bare hands, and in some miraculous way manages to get her close enough to shore for a firefighter, now also in the water and with a lifeline attached, to grab her and pull her to safety.

Lenny Skutnik was at the time twenty-nine years old. He held a job as a printing and distribution assistant for the Congressional Budget Office.

On 26 January 1982 Lenny was the guest of honour at the State of the Union address, invited by President Ronald Reagan. He sat next to First Lady Nancy Reagan as the leader of the free world praised Lenny for his bravery, and he received a standing ovation from the entire assembled audience. During the following weeks Lenny received more than 1,600 letters thanking him for his good deed.

By showing leadership on that tragic day in January 1982 Lenny had restored our faith that we human beings actually do want to help each other. Bystander apathy is no natural law; it can be overcome. It *is* possible for a normal person, without special skills, to step up as a leader even in an extreme situation like this. Lenny made us believe in ourselves again.

2. At scale

The lessons we can learn from the tragic murder of Kitty Genovese, the bravery of Lenny Skutnik and the experiments done on the bystander effect, go a long way to explaining leadership both at a very personal level and on a much bigger scale. Fundamentally it's the same dynamic at play: either we step up or we don't. Leadership is a choice, not a position.

However, as we've seen in these two stories, we tend to gravitate towards apathy. This makes stepping up the counter-intuitive choice. As such, we

Lenny Skutnik's bravery did not pass unnoticed. True leadership rarely does.

must continuously work to build up a leader's mind-set, and be ever ready to step up.

Let's see what happens 'at scale', when bystander apathy becomes the standard in organizations, re-sulting in a greater number of victims.

In March 2003 Zhang Linwei and his wife Liu Li felt truly blessed as they brought their newborn baby girl, Rongrong, with them from the hospital to the family's little home in Wangzhuang, a small village about midway between Beijing and Hong Kong, China.

As first-time parents the couple was very pre-occupied with their baby's health, and since her crying gradually became quieter Zhang and Liu got concerned. A few days later, as little Rongrong was growing a disproportionally big head and an abnormally small mouth, the couple took their daughter to the hospital. Zhang recalls: 'The doc-tors said they couldn't treat my baby. They had re-ceived numerous similar cases.' Full of fear and uncertainty the parents took their beloved baby home, and did their best to heal her. One fateful day in August 2003, the five-month-old Rongrong took her last breath. Zhang and Liu were heart-broken.

This is not the intro to a Hollywood movie about outbreaks, pandemics and incurable diseases. Instead it's a true story of a massive failure of leadership on multiple levels, and the devastating death of more than sixty babies in Wangzhuang and the neighbouring villages.

Meet melamine. You probably have it in your home, either as a countertop, as dinnerware, in laminate flooring, or in your whiteboard. For these purposes, a rather innocent material. Not so much when used as an ingredient in baby-milk powder. Rongrong died because the milk her parents so eagerly fed her had no more nutritional value than water. 'Our baby starved to death,' Zhang explains. The young couple's mistake was to trust the government-approved, and supermarket-endorsed, locally produced milk-powder brand.

We are not dealing with one misguided employee going rogue and endangering thousands of babies single-handedly. What shocked the world back in 2004 was to learn that 141 factories from twenty-one different companies were using similar practices, adding melamine to fake the protein levels, as the techniques used for testing cannot tell the difference between nitrogen in melamine and natural protein. This fraud made it possible for the companies to sell a product labelled as baby milk, but containing only 6 per cent of the vitamins, minerals and protein needed for a growing infant.

Intake of melamine is also known to cause severe urinary problems and kidney damage, and is universally banned in food production.

Truth is said to be stranger than fiction, and in this case it is certainly a lot sadder: in 2008 new incidents came to light, and this time on a nationwide scale. China reported 300,000 victims of bogus baby-food products, with 54,000 infants being hospitalized. Dozens of high-ranking government officials were charged with corruption, looking the other way whilst corporate greed was allowed to flourish. This time two leaders from the worst-behaving companies were executed. Which of course didn't bring any of the babies back.

You might be living a long way from China, and thinking that failures of this magnitude could never happen in the Western world. Rest assured, they do. And, one can only wonder how many fall into the trap of being passive bystanders.

Suffice it to say, we need more of us to become leaders. In our everyday lives, driving in traffic, living in communities, shopping at malls. We need to unlock our leadership potential whatever form of organization we find ourselves in: from our local sports club, to all types of companies, NGOs and government agencies. Just as importantly we must step up as *leaders of one*, as masters of our own lives,

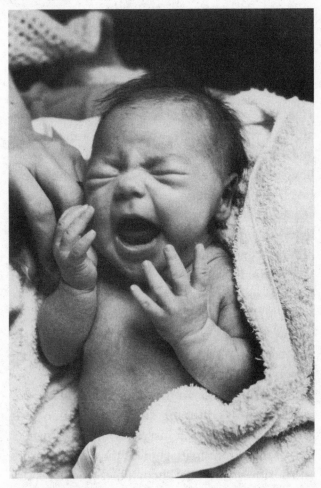
Some stakeholders in our leadership are more vulnerable than others.

in addition to being trustworthy family members, friends and neighbours.

3. This book

How to Be a Leader is based on the premise that we all have the potential to be wise, compassionate and impactful leaders. This is not a book about how to manage people or how to climb the corporate ladder – although promotion is a natural consequence of good leadership. Rather, we will shed light on some universal principles that underpin different shapes and forms of leadership, with the aim of finally situating leadership in the broader human context.

In this book, we look to the future, being aware of how fast our world and collective consciousness are evolving. As our context changes, so must our leadership practices.

What follows is an invitation to bring a wider range of ideas, thinking and practices into your leadership, rather than just a narrow set of principles hailing from management theory, economics and business studies. Although these are necessary elements as well, they are amply covered in the existing leadership literature.

As you will see, we draw on leading-edge research from our academic partner, Ashridge Executive Education, part of Hult International Business School, which has six research centres, each focussing on specific areas: action research, business and sustainability, coaching, leadership training, strategic management and executive development.

Rather than putting forth a set theoretical framework, this book was conceived as a companion to take with you on your leadership journey. It holds wisdom from the wonderful leaders we interviewed, stories from our own lives and experiences, insights from cultural studies and timeless wisdom from some of the most loved philosophers.

The stories and metaphors are meant to illustrate a hero's journey – whether leading through crisis, living with uncertainty or turning a painful past into a platform for impactful leadership. These stories are told as precisely as possible, as we intend for them to evoke emotion as well as our uniquely human capacity to imagine. They are meant to move you, inspire you and remind you that every moment is an occasion for leadership. Perhaps you will recognize yourself in some of these accounts of challenges, growth, forgiveness and acceptance. We hope they will serve as lessons and prepare you to respond to challenges and situations you encounter as a leader.

How to Be a Leader is divided into three parts: 'You', 'You + Others', and 'Shadow'. The first part is about building a strong foundation for your leadership, and that process starts with you. How can we lead others if we ourselves don't know who we are, and where we are going?

In the second part we focus on lessons and practices around relating to others. What we can achieve on our own is very limited, whilst it's often been shown that a strong team, big or small, can change the world in significant ways.

In the final part we look at some shadow elements, which are highly impactful in leadership. In defining moments we often fall short, thereby compromising everything that the best version of our self has put so much effort into creating. Here, we explore crisis, uncertainty, failure and the ego.

Across these three parts we present you with the twelve strongest leadership lessons we have encountered during our work. This list is by no means exhaustive. There is a lot more that could be said about leadership. We carefully selected what we considered to be the most salient and often neglected aspects of what it means to be a leader.

4. The story of us

Who are we to write this book, and why do we care?

Cosmina grew up in Romania, during arguably one of the most oppressive Communist regimes, under Ceauşsescu's dictatorship. She experienced first-hand what we today consider to be history's biggest experiment with centralized leadership. At the age of eighteen, thanks to an unexpected act of kindness, Cosmina had the opportunity to study in the United States and left Romania eight years after the revolution that overthrew its dictators.

Arrived in the land of her dreams, Cosmina sat in a twelve-student classroom at the third oldest academic institution in the United States, the prestigious St John's College in Annapolis, Maryland. Four years of discussing Homer, Plato, Aristotle, Hegel, Kant and just about everyone that has revolutionized Western thought prepared her to look for excellence that is divorced from status, credentials and power-dynamics.

After eleven years in the US she moved to London to get her Masters of Science degree in Environment and International Development. Then in 2013 she joined forces with a small team in Washington DC to create a start-up accelerator with the aim of building more new-era businesses from the ground up, whilst training more aware and conscious leaders.

She brings in new dimensions to leadership, gained from her current role of eco-system builder, start-up coach and catalyst for changing the way business is practised.

The Nordic countries are said to have found their 'third way', creating a welfare state without diminishing the right to pursue individual ambitions. This is the context in which Martin grew up, and with a few exceptions he is very fond of the Danish values and culture. Where Martin comes from, happiness is a big deal, and work–life balance is for everyone who wants it. He is proud of the fact that a disproportionally high number of the world's greatest scientists, thinkers, athletes and innovators continue to hail from Denmark.

Martin started out at the age of eighteen as an entrepreneur, and in hindsight a terrible leader. Luckily, his first attempts failed and as a frustrated young man Martin had to surrender, take a degree, and get a corporate job. He spent fifteen painful months as a McKinsey consultant travelling the world, and then a couple of exciting years helping a successful Danish entrepreneur with his companies. Then he was finally ready to give entrepreneurship another go.

In 2006, Martin co-founded Rainmaking, a start-up factory where there are six owners all with co-CEO leadership responsibility for the hundreds of team members they now have working across thirty countries.

In addition to their own start-ups, they are running three co-working spaces, Rainmaking Lofts, housing a total of nearly 1,000 entrepreneurs, as well as managing investments in more than 300 start-ups all around the world via their accelerator, Startupbootcamp.

In 2013, Martin published his first book, *Winning Without Losing*, co-authored with Jordan Milne, which was awarded Management Book of the Year in the New Manager category by CMI, Henley Business School and the British Library. The book went on to become an international bestseller, now out in fifteen languages and thirty-five countries. In 2015 Martin published *The Great Idea*, an entrepreneurial fairy tale for children, because he feels strongly about giving the next generation a better introduction to entrepreneurship than what has so far been the norm.

Today, a big part of Rainmaking's activities is to help large corporates become better at innovation.

Martin feels that he has come full circle, from start-ups to corporates, to start-ups and back to corporates again. Building a bridge between the two worlds is the leadership task he nowadays feels called to take on.

This book project seemed to us to require both of our skill-sets and backgrounds. Cosmina is the philosophical voice, Martin is the practical entrepreneur. We both have leadership experience from multiple angles and care deeply about the topic.

We are convinced that leadership is evolving, and will keep evolving, to reach higher and more sustainable levels than we have witnessed in the past. This is not only natural, it's also necessary. As such, we appreciate the opportunity to share our voices, and the voices of those we have interviewed, and to play a role in the conversation about what comes next. Speaking of voices, we are growing weary of talking about ourselves in the third person. So in the twelve chapters that follow, we will be taking turns narrating. First Martin, then Cosmina, and so on.

We hope you will enjoy the journey.

I. You

At the forecourt of the Temple of Apollo in Delphi, Greece, the inscribed words *Know Thyself* have been inspiring visitors for millennia. For anyone with leadership aspirations, these words should be more than ancient-time graffiti. Leadership starts with you; there's no way around it.

We begin Part One with a story about discovering one's purpose, or *raison d'être*. A moving testimony of hope and of assurance that every one of us is here to do a job, including the protagonist of our story, who grew up being told that he was stupid and would never amount to anything. If you connect your leadership with your purpose – that thing which ignites you and makes you come alive – you will become a beacon for those around you.

In the second chapter we look at the body – our physical form – as a precious and wise container for consciousness, and a finely tuned instrument to express our leadership. By cultivating awareness of the way in which we care for and inhabit our bodies, we become open to a whole new level of wisdom and insight beyond what our conscious mind can offer. In this chapter our aim is to invite you to integrate head-based intellect, heart-based values and gut-based instincts.

Curiosity about yourself, about the world around you, and a continued quest for knowledge is the topic of Chapter 3. Here we make the case that curiosity is a powerful leadership tool. Add it to your toolbox and get ready be amazed.

The world needs leaders that genuinely seek to live in harmony with nature. 'Understanding our place in the cosmos is a vital leadership awareness for this century,' says Chris Nichols, co-director of the Ashridge Masters in Sustainability and Responsibility programme. In Chapter 4, we invite you to see yourself as an integral part of nature, to learn from her 3.8 billion years of evolution, and to frame your leadership from a position of oneness with nature.

A leader's job is to become a touchstone of wisdom, awareness and compassion. And it is the work we do on ourselves that becomes the cauldron from which our leadership emerges.

1. Is There Something You Really, Really Care About?

If you visit Glenville National School's website you will find a lot of pictures of smiling children. At an Easter raffle, on a bus ride, during a school play. Under the Policies tab you can read an anti-bullying statement, outlining how the school secures a good environment for all children:

> The school attempts at all times to foster a positive attitude in pupils towards fellow pupils and the education process in general. We also try to encourage a positive self-image in the individual child.

It's difficult to know whether the website is a fair representation of the realities facing the students at this school, in the southern part of Ireland, today. Back in the 1990s it surely was a very different experience. Former pupil John Sweeney and his mother have the court's word for it.

John was beaten most days at school. When it got too bad his mother kept him home for days or weeks, so he could heal emotionally and physically. She brought the matter to the school principal many times. He laughed at her. The principal was one of those doing the beating. As was his wife, the vice principal. From the age of seven, John was regularly hit with rulers, fists, or whatever was within reach. He was abused by the teachers who were supposed to educate, protect and inspire him. They repeatedly told him that he was 'thick, stupid and wouldn't amount to anything'.

Children learn fast and it didn't take long before everyone in the class knew that if you were angry, you could just beat John Sweeney. When he was in sixth class some of the kids from fifth class wanted to have their go as well. Being a year younger than John they decided to gang up, and attacked him from behind in a school corridor. One of them got free access to John's neck and hammered away. That day the eleven-year-old John nearly died.

The incident only met with mockery from the school leadership, so in the deepest despair a mother can face, unable to protect her son, Mary Sweeney pressed legal charges. It would take seven more years of injustice and suffering before the school had to give in and pay a symbolic settlement to John Sweeney, at that time an eighteen-year-old plumber.

'My mother did everything she could. She has always been very kind to me. But we were working class, and as she took legal action we lost the last few friends we had in the town. Everyone said that we were disgracing Glenville. Even our own family members believed that we brought shame on the family name,' John recalls.

Mary Sweeney's job was to drive the local school bus, and almost every morning during those years she would be greeted by a load of slurs written on the bus about her son, herself and the rest of the family.

'There was a period, in my first year of secondary school, where things had cleared up a bit, and I actually had some friends that I was really enjoying spending time with,' John tells. 'But on my thirteenth birthday there was a setback as a group of ten to twelve boys decided to beat me up again, as a sort of birthday present. They got me so bad that the school actually expelled a few of them. But that only made things worse since everyone at the school – students, teachers, parents – held me to blame for the misfortune of those expelled,' John continues. 'I literally didn't have a friend in the whole world.'

John tells me all this in a very kind, unapologetic, matter-of-fact way. Still, if it weren't for what John is doing today, and the genuine smile on his face, this wouldn't be much more than just another sad story. Instead, meeting John has been the most inspiring and empowering encounter I have had this year. It has also been living proof of the wisdom in the words of Holocaust survivor and best-selling author Viktor E. Frankl: 'What is to give light must first endure burning.'

Now, there was no quick fix for John Sweeney. He needed healing and it didn't come easy. Luckily, at age seventeen he met a girl who didn't know anything about his status as the local outcast. She saw John for what he was, as worthy of love as anyone, and the sweetest guy she had ever met. Erin and John are now married, and have four children. Their birthdays are on the exact same day, with Erin being one year older than John.

'When Erin saw how I was still being bullied, she urged for us to get away from Glenville. We did, and that saved me,' John tells.

John knew that he didn't deserve all the beating he had received, but the being 'thick, stupid and wouldn't amount to anything' part would prove especially hard to shake. He worked as a plumber, only because that was the occupation his abusive teachers had told him would be the one job he might be capable of doing.

The truth was, however, that John was a terrible plumber. He just wasn't cut out for it.

John of course knew that he was misplaced, and year after year he tried to get into college. With all the days away from school his academic record was far from impressive, and he was encouraged to demonstrate his determination by doing social and voluntary work. He joined the local Scouts, and worked with victims of bullying, helping them as much as he could. The effort was worthwhile for John and the children he supported, but no matter how hard he tried, John failed to get accepted into college.

Finally, after ten years, John gave up the plumbing profession, as well as the college dream. For two years he had random jobs, but then he ran into unemployment and didn't seem to be able to get going again. Closing in on his thirtieth birthday, feeling completely useless, depression caught up with him.

Then something unexpected happened.

John's own words from a recent article in the *Huffington Post* explain it best:

On 27 March 2013, I was stressed, unable to sleep, and worried about putting food on the table. I was an unemployed husband and father who had made it this far, through following the direction of others. Now I had responsibilities, no work, nobody to tell me how to make a change for the better and was terrified by the uncertainty. It was yet another night that I just couldn't sleep. It was then, at 2.30 a.m., that I first read about a tradition born in the working class cafes of Naples, Italy, where people would advance purchase a coffee for someone in need.

Mark Twain said that the two most important days in your life are the day that you are born, and the day that you discover why. In that moment, sitting at my computer in the dark, I had discovered my 'why'. In a moment of inspiration, I set up a Facebook page called *Suspended Coffees*, encouraging people to commit to paying it forward through simple acts of kindness.[1]

Reading this might make you think two things:

Firstly, 'This guy doesn't seem as dim as his teachers claimed.' And, secondly, 'Yeah, I too once

set up a Facebook page in a moment of craziness.'
(I know I did . . .)

Only John wasn't crazy. Or if he was, so are the
295,000 people that have since Liked his page –
and the over 2,000 cafes and coffee houses that
have signed up to be part of his movement. The
concept is simple: if you are feeling generous you
can pay for an extra cup of coffee (or anything else)
at one of the cafes and coffee houses that have
joined, and then someone in need can be served for
free. This is a frictionless and powerful way to demonstrate kindness. And it does wonders for local
communities. John's page is overflowing with wonderful examples of kindness and what it does to
the human spirit.

The movement is totally free and open to everyone. John clearly didn't do this to make money. In
fact he stills struggles to put food on the table.
When asked why he chooses to spend all of his waking hours doing a job he doesn't get paid to do, he
answers without hesitation 'because I have to do it'.
At first that can seem silly, but now that you know
John's history, you can probably appreciate why his
new career choice makes perfect sense to him. John
really, really cares about kindness.

I have met maybe a dozen leaders of movements, and I have often walked away disappointed.

Whilst their work has been important and admirable, I didn't feel comfortable with their motives. They would trademark and copyright everything. They would enjoy being on stage a bit too much. Totally normal needs and wants like attention, power and possessions usually strike me as just as central to most movements as the mission they share publicly. With John Sweeney and his Suspended Coffees I don't get that feeling at all. Here's why.

Throughout the conversations I have had with John he has never asked me for anything. More than anyone I know, John has internalized the wisdom in 'ask not what others can do for you, but what you can do for others'. When John does you a favour (for instance he does a lot of coaching for free), he only asks for one thing in return: that you turn around and do someone else a favour.

When I asked John how many cafes have joined his movement, he told me he couldn't really know because he just encourages them to start doing the work. They don't need to use his Facebook page or the stickers he has had produced. John hasn't (at least not yet) been corrupted by the idea of building an empire. The cause itself is what matters to him.

John walks the talk. And not just when the cameras are on.

Hearing John's story, and writing this chapter, I couldn't stop myself from getting a feeling of anger in my chest. I found myself looking up the name of the former school principal, and for a few moments I even toyed with the idea of giving him a call to ask him how he could possibly have been so wicked back then (shame on me). John, on the other hand, is not the least preoccupied with anger or lust for retaliation. He might have been once, I can't really know, but today he is fully focussed on kindness as the way to heal the world (and his world).

Although he didn't get the best of starts, John is now leading a big and growing movement that inspires thousands of people every day. Some of his updates reach as many as 1.5 million readers. People he encounters on his path write articles and blog posts about the impact John Sweeney has had on their lives. He is doing TEDx talks, and is regularly being flown across the Atlantic to tell his story. Without having to ask for their help, John currently has a handful of people working full-time, for free, on spreading the message of kindness and growing the movement.

The best leaders in the world find what they really care about, and almost everything else flows from this point.

But many of us live in a way that is out of

alignment with our true purpose. This gives us an uneasy feeling that can be so hard to shake – 'Is this really all there is?' We do the job, and yet we long for something more meaningful. The challenging thing is that meaning is different for all of us. I have never been bullied, so whilst I can appreciate John's mission, I could never make it mine. My own deep connection is with entrepreneurship, and I have made that my leadership platform.

What John's story tells us is that there is a deeper, more personal place where leadership can and should start from. His story is moving whilst also being a clear pointer that any one of us can start a movement, lead from the front, or change something in the world, by looking for clues in even the most painful of our life's events. Whilst John's story may not be your story, we can all be inspired by his ability to sit in this alchemical fire and emerge on the other side a brighter leader.

The questions we invite you to ask yourself are:

- Is there something I really care about?
- Have I managed to make that thing the centre of my universe?

It's not easy, but if you can get to an unequivocal 'yes' to both questions, leadership, impact and prog-

Finding our purpose requires stillness and solitude.

ress will follow almost automatically. John is not the best manager or operator I have ever met, far from it. He started completely from nothing, without education and without a 'friend in the world'. Within two years he went from reading an article in a moment of despair, to inspiring millions of people across the world. Just imagine what you can do, with your skills, resources and network! Leadership truly is for everyone.

Practice
Carve out four hours for yourself. Go out in nature. Sit on a rock. Think about your life and your most radical and painful experiences up to this point. When have you been burnt? When have you had strong feelings of pain, beauty or both?

Now ask yourself again: *Is there something that I really, really care about?*

If the answer is no, and you are happy and content with your life – then all's good. If however you are feeling a lack of meaning in your life, then dig deeper.

If the answer is yes, then this might be the second most important day of your life.

2. Mind the Body

As I navigated my way to the departure gate, boarding my forty-fifth flight in eight months, I wondered . . . was this last-minute, long-haul trip really necessary? Have I rescheduled all the meetings and appointments I had on my calendar for the rest of the week? Better question: how will my body cope with all this travel and jet lag?

For context, I live and work in three countries on two different continents. It's easy to see how this commute can take a toll on my body. Perhaps extensive travel isn't your plight. Maybe your methods of 'abusing' your body are spending too much time sitting at your desk, too little sleep, too many hangovers after the office happy hours, or not enough movement and exercise. Whatever it is, we all know the story. Too much to do, too little time, but we feel that we can just push through. Sure, that may work for a while. But we really only begin to pay attention to our body when crisis hits. At least that was the case for me, when, a few years ago

I found myself grappling with the news that I would need to have cervical spine surgery.

It was in my journey through finding alternative healing modalities that I first began to realize how little time we spend minding our bodies. Steamrolled by the myriad of tasks, meetings, obligations and commitments we place on ourselves, we very often revert to treating our bodies, in the words of Sir Ken Robinson, 'as a form of transport for our heads'.[1]

As such, we must be intentional in finding ways to counter modernity's assault on our physical form. This is all the more important for leaders. It should come as no surprise that whatever we say or do as leaders sends a message to our organization, community or any other type of group we are leading. Our relationship with our body is no exception. The way we care for our physical form, and the way we carry ourselves, either inspires and commands respect or provokes judgment and criticism from those around.

Historically, the approach to leadership training has been conceptual—in other words, all in the head. What frameworks, what skills, what classroom-based instruction would prove most effective in training and developing new leaders? By now we should admit that thinking and conceptualizing our way into a new way of leading simply won't work. New-paradigm leadership requires congruency of heart, body, mind and soul.

Leadership, therefore, must be embodied. But for this to happen, we must reacquaint ourselves with the wonder that is our physical form.

In this chapter, we'll explore the body through three different lenses: 1) body as temple or vehicle which houses our consciousness; 2) body as sage, looking at the intelligence inherent in our body and biology; and 3) body as expression, and the concept of presence, which we feel is vital to being a leader in today's world. By the end of the chapter you will gain a better understanding of how important the body is in carrying out your leadership.

1. Body as temple

We live in a time of a mass-scale exodus from our bodies and a homelessness of spirit. This is a global malady, but particularly acute in the Western world. Of course it's not all our fault. We have inherited a great divide, a deep-rooted notion of separation of spirit and mind from matter. This misconception of separation has its roots deep in the human story, back when conflict first arose between church and science, when any new discovery that challenged the church's authority was deemed blasphemous. In addition, René Descartes's argument for dualism further contributed to our propensity for treating our bodies as machines.

Fortunately we have evolved past Descartes's dualism and we are gradually awakening to just how integrated mind and matter really are.

Let's look at some practical things you can do to develop the body of a leader. By now you know that I am not referring to body language. Rather, my invitation is to notice the cumulative effects of your life choices and make the necessary adjustments so that you can develop the body you can come home to.

What follows is by no means a complete list, as reams could be written just on this topic. Take these words as gentle reminders that we can and must do our best to look after the temple we've been given.

Sleep

Although the science is still in its infancy, there's a raft of research on sleep. To get a better sense of what happens when we sleep and why sleep is vital to leadership, we discussed the topic with Dr Vicki Culpin, Dean of Faculty and Director of Research at Ashridge Business School. Vicki has been re-

Descartes. Sometimes it's a good idea to get out of your mind and into your body. Even for the biggest thinkers.

searching the implications of sleep in leadership practice for decades.

'There's been a myth, certainly up until a few years ago, that when we sleep we're unconscious, that the brain ceases activity and we go into almost a coma state. That isn't the case at all. There are a lot of different stages to sleep and lots of things happen in each stage,' explains Vicki.

Here's why sleep really matters, and why it's important for leaders:

'Sleep is vital for *memory consolidation*,' says Vicki. If we consume information prior to going to sleep for a minimum of an hour and a half (because that's how long it takes to go through an entire cycle of sleep), this enables our brain to consolidate learning and we retain that information for a longer period of time.

It is also extremely important for *cell regeneration and rejuvenation*. A recent study conducted by Dr Maiken Nedergaard, a Danish biologist studying sleep function at the University of Rochester's medical school, shows that whilst we sleep there is an increase in the amount of cerebral spinal fluid moving around the synapses in the brain, which basically plays the part of a mental janitor, doing a deep clean of the dead and dying cells.[2]

Health and well-being are also greatly impacted

by our sleep habits. 'It's really important to note that sleep is hugely individual. It's difficult to work out cause and effect; however, chronic poor sleep has been shown to relate to some types of cancer, obesity, cardiovascular disease, and early onset of adult diabetes, to name a few,' says Vicki. If you're in doubt about the amount of sleep you should aim for each night, note that there is some consensus on the topic. To promote optimal health, adults should sleep seven hours, or more ideally, every night.[3]

There's something to the old saying 'sleep on it'. Eureka moments, the ability to join unconnected dots or bring about a novel solution, are more likely to happen after a good night's sleep. 'This suggests that at night the brain is also filing memories and looking at the big picture,' says Vicki. Sleep therefore plays an important role in *discernment*.

Self-care

It would serve us to begin to see our physical form as a finely engineered home for our consciousness, and treat it as such.

If, for example, I choose to drink and obliterate myself at my company's Christmas party, I will not only make an infelicitous impression on those around me, but it becomes impossible for consciousness to flow through my system. You needn't take my word for it. In a letter to his mother, Nietzsche describes an incident with alcohol as 'one of the most unpleasant and painful incidents I have been responsible for', and he did little to conceal his irritation with his fellow students at Bonn and Leipzig universities for their love of alcohol and their 'beery materialism'.[4]

As we evolve our consciousness, our body also evolves and refines itself. I experienced this first-hand whilst at an intense meditation retreat. At the beginning of the retreat, the body was nothing more than a source of pain and frustration. The early-morning rise followed by long hours of sitting had me in tears by the second day. All I wanted to do was run away. But, with the right nutrition and hydration, rest, movement and stretching, the body slowly began to assist and expand rather than impede my experience.

Check in with yourself and see where you are now. However treacherous the journey to changing unhealthy habits may seem, whatever discontent we may feel at our genetic inheritance, change is possible and damage can be reversed. It truly does not matter where we start. What's important is that we acknowledge where we are, accept and love ourselves exactly as we are. And from that place, begin to make healthier choices. In doing so, we ensure that the physical form is there as a vessel for our leadership.

Movement
As we begin to honour and work with the body from the inside out, we increase our awareness of the way the body moves, of the space we take up both physically and energetically.

'On a fundamental level, life is movement,' my business coach used to say, encouraging me to find my movement practice. My movement is dance, particularly meditative dance practices like 5Rhythms. For me, dance evokes reflection and releases the energy of emotion, allowing it to flow right through.

I invite you to find your movement, whatever that may be, and begin to explore your relationship with the space within and around you.

2. Body as sage

'My primary process of perceiving is muscular and visual,' said Albert Einstein.

A sage, or *sophos* in Ancient Greek, is someone

who has attained the wisdom a philosopher seeks. There is more wisdom in our bones and in our biology than we'll ever fully comprehend. It has taken eons of evolutionary intelligence to arrive at where we are today. It is time to harness this wisdom and bring it into our leadership.

You may have come across statements such as 'the body does not lie'.[5] But just how intelligent is the human body?

Science tells us that we have three brains residing inside our skulls, each with its own anatomy and circuitry. The neocortex, the newest brain in our evolution, is also known as the thinking brain. Amongst other functions, our neocortex gathers information, processes language, and makes synaptic connections. The limbic brain is also known as the emotional brain because emotion is a chemical released in the limbic brain. Dr Joe Dispenza suggests that this is the brain that allows you to remember finishing a marathon, seeing a beautiful sunset, or your first kiss.[6] The third brain, the cerebellum, or reptilian brain, plays a major role in motor learning and motor control. It deals with survival issues, and is the seat of our subconscious mind.

However, the field of neuroscience has revealed findings that support the notion that the seat of intelligence isn't limited to the three brains inside our skull.

In 1991, neurocardiology researcher J. Andrew Armour introduced a startling concept that we have a complex neural network – in other words, a functional brain – inside our hearts.[7] This came to be known as the *cardiac brain*. It turns out, the heart, which is the first organ to form in embryogenesis, maintains a continuous two-way dialogue with the brains inside our skulls and with the rest of the body.[8]

Then, in 1998, neurobiologist Dr Michael Gershon revealed the result of over a decade of research suggesting that our gut also contains a fully functional neural network, which came to be known as the *enteric brain* or the *gut brain*.[9] According to Dr Gershon, the gut brain is a neurohormonal warehouse which utilizes the same type of neurotransmitters found in the brain residing inside our skulls. So, it behoves us to pay attention to those I-know-it-in-my-gut feelings.

Moreover, researchers in the emerging field of epigenetics – arguing against genetic determinism – suggest that every living cell in our body is an intelligent 'programmable chip' whose behaviour and genetic activity is controlled primarily by environmental signals, not just by genes.[10] Although the jury is still out on the exact number, it is estimated that there are over 37.2 trillion cells in the human body.[11] These smart cells live harmoniously under one roof (the healthy human body) in a constant conversation with each other and the environment around us.

From the work of Dr David Hawkins, we know that the human central nervous system has 'an exquisitely sensitive capacity to differentiate between life-supporting and life-destructive patterns'.[12] In other words, your body has a 'yes' or 'no' response to everything around you.

Imagine how powerful your leadership will be when you bring this vast intelligence of your physical form into all of your leadership decisions. Once you learn to understand your body's 'yes' and 'no' responses, how easy would you say it would be for others around you to mislead or deceive you? What would your leadership look like once you've mastered the ability to bring into alignment all of your brains: the head brain, heart brain and gut brain?

3. Embodied presence

We should by now feel really good about the fact that our body contains so much intelligence. *Wis-*

dom, however, is determined by our awareness, and by our ability to align heart, mind and body.

American author, poet and dancer Maya Angelou famously said, 'I've learned that people will forget what you said, people will forget what you did, but people will never forget how you made them feel.'

We communicate well before we open our mouths and engage our voice boxes. And these subtle non-verbal messages typically register in our limbic (emotional) brain and linger in our memory. I once worked with someone who would walk into a meeting, and it felt as though the air was literally sucked out of the room. Restless and irritated, there was no space around him, and the tension was palpable.

So, being aware of how we inhabit the body, of our physical carriage and the quality of our presence, is an important skill in life, not just in leadership.

What is presence? Betty Sue Flowers is an expert on the topic and a co-author of *Presence: Exploring Profound Change in People, Organizations and Society*. In our interview, she describes presence as 'a kind of deep listening for a future that wants to emerge.' Betty Sue explains that when you are in a group, by staying open and not controlling you can create a high-intensity field, become really in synch with your team, and together you can perceive what needs to happen next. 'That's really a magical feeling', says Betty Sue. 'The closest analogy is to the way artists create art. They're always struggling with some aspect of the form – what's the right meter for a poem, the best canvas for a painting. They have to step back, listen and be open to sensing what wants to emerge.'

Presence is therefore a cultivation of depth and awareness, a way of being, a surrendering to the present moment. By holding this space of intense listening and sensing, as a leader you will be able to create more space for those around you, allowing them to be more creative. This happens because the depth of your presence will resonate with those around you. It's up to you, as a leader, to ensure that this effect is a constructive one.

Practice
This chapter calls for several practices including getting your seven hours of sleep per night, finding your movement, assessing lifestyle choices, and more. All of which are critical to embodying leadership. As with the previous chapter, these lessons can be

learnt by anyone, regardless of their social status or their place on the employment hi-erarchy. What's important is that we develop a body that will assist and enhance our leadership.

3. Unleash Your Curiosity

At a fundamental level, all progress starts with curiosity – with different versions of the basic question: how can this be done in a better way? Without curiosity we wouldn't have smart phones, the International Space Station, Ben & Jerry's ice cream or selfie sticks.

Leaders make a reality happen that wouldn't have happened otherwise. The best of them keep their creative powers from childhood, they continue to learn with an open mind, and we marvel at their ability to ask unexpected questions and reimagine the reality that the rest of us have grown to accept as the status quo.

The truth is that this ability doesn't need to be scarce. It has very little to do with IQ or any innate capability. It's rather a habit, a choice, and a skill that we can practise and improve. Curiosity is in fact at all times readily available to all of us. Unleashing it might be what it takes to propel our leadership to the next level.

In this chapter we will make a case for curiosity as a leadership tool, and give you specific ideas for how to practise and expand your capacity for curiosity. For inspiration we will share an example of a remarkable Danish leader who, by using his curiosity, is transforming two of the most conservative institutions: education and politics. But, like most things, curiosity has a dark side, and we will address that as well, so that you can steer clear of the pitfalls.

First, imagine a world without curiosity. When we engage in that thought experiment it quickly becomes clear that such a world would be incredibly boring. Tomorrow would be more or less like today. Forever. Whilst that might seem comforting to those of us who feel overwhelmed by the VUCA (Vulnerability, Uncertainty, Complexity, Ambiguity) premises of the modern world, I think most of us will agree that living the same day over and over again would eventually kill our human spirit. Inmates do it, and we call it punishment. A lot of people do it when retired – and those are the ones that seem to be getting ten years older during their first year of retirement. In order to thrive, most of us need surroundings and circumstances that change, develop and ideally improve. Our curiosity is what makes tomorrow interesting.

Even when we don't understand it all, curiosity makes our lives richer.

Another great thing about curiosity is that it is the foundation for learning. Children are the most curious of our species, and they are the fastest learners. Likewise for us adults, every time we ask a question and listen to the answer we learn something. When we share our own thinking, or viewpoints that we have been committed to for years, we might at best influence someone else or sound smart. But we will surely not expand our minds or learn anything new.

If, in your leadership, you encounter some level of feeling stuck, overwhelmed or even depressed, curiosity can be the fast track out. You might get advice like 'try not to worry so much', 'time is short, so enjoy your life' or 'be grateful for all you have'. But those things are virtually impossible to do when feeling really down. Even in the toughest moments we can find something, however tiny it may be, to be curious about.

Interviewed by Jonathan Fields for his podcast, the GoodLifeProject, Elizabeth Gilbert, author of the iconic bestseller *Eat, Pray, Love*, shared what had been her own way out of a deep depression. For days on end she had found herself curled up in a corner of her couch, crying helplessly. She was really sad – and felt unable to get back on track. Then one day her curiosity led her to ask what if she wasn't in fact totally helpless, what if she could alter something about this picture? She couldn't stop crying, but she wondered if she could stand on one leg whilst sobbing – instead of being on the couch. It turned out that she could. What might seem like a small change, felt like a massive win for Elizabeth.

The next day she did it again, and this time she suddenly found herself laughing at how ridiculous she must have looked, standing there on one leg in the middle of the living room, crying. This became the turning point in her depression, and with curiosity by her side she took baby steps that eventually brought her back to living not only a good life, but in fact a great and enormously creative life.

Now let's look at another leader who embodies curiosity. Uffe Elbæk started out doing art projects and creative entrepreneurial endeavours of the sort that the establishment had a hard time understanding. In the autumn of 1989 Uffe and his friends arranged for more than 2,000 young Danes to enter into the Soviet Union, at the time one of the most totalitarian and closed places on the planet. The plan was to organize a rock concert in front of Moscow University. The Danish rock band Sort Sol was one of the names on stage, and was subsequently banned in the communist country, where rock concerts were just as rare as democratic rights. For the young campaigners the experience was breathtaking, dramatic, and boosted their self-confidence.

Afterwards the group asked themselves this simple question: 'What kind of education could prepare more people to do what we did?' They quickly realized that such an education did not exist; in fact they couldn't find anything suitable anywhere in the world.

Starting from a point of curiosity, Uffe and his friends, with their characteristic flair for action, went on to launch their own school that they named KaosPilot University. Their mission was to create a holistic experience for the students, where body, mind and spirit were equally applied and developed, and where creativity, freethinking and entrepreneurship were at the heart of everything they did. Students shouldn't be kept on the bench, listening to long monologues on abstract theories; instead, they should be out practising how to create the future. At the same time the education was heavily inspired by philosophy, art and science, making it an incredibly insightful as well as refreshingly action-oriented environment.

Today, KaosPilot has been recognized by *Businessweek* as one of the best design schools in the world, and Fast Company has named it in its Start-up Leagues Big 10. They have expanded internationally and are co-creating education programmes together with renowned institutions like the Royal College of Art in London and the Hong Kong Design Centre. Half of their alumni are in leadership positions, and another 33 per cent have started their own businesses. I have met numerous KaosPilots, and it's remarkable how they all share the same can-do attitude. They are creative, curious, self-confident and action-oriented.

After having once again successfully made his own utopia become a reality, Uffe Elbæk started wondering about what it would take to transform a whole country to become more vibrant, open-minded and inspired. From the sidelines I witnessed him go into politics, and like most other Danes, I have to admit I didn't predict he would last very long. We all know that politics is brutal, and from my outsider perspective Uffe didn't seem cynical or thick-skinned enough to have staying power in the political menagerie.

When I interviewed Uffe for this book, he recalled standing on a street corner in Copenhagen when one of his volunteers asked him this question: 'Why don't we start a *new* political party?' His first reaction was 'no way', but over the following days, curiosity kicked in and he watched himself return to the thought. Shortly after the seed was planted, he sat down and wrote a manifesto, and systematically worked through his favourite eight-step process for concept development, analysing the project via multiple lenses.

On 27 November 2013 Uffe Elbæk together with Josefine Fock presented the ideas and thoughts behind a new political party in Denmark, named The Alternative. Uffe explained to the press how The Alternative had a value statement and a manifesto, but not yet a political programme. The reason being that they were against the traditional top-down structure, and had involvement as a key value – so instead of merely presenting a political programme they thereby extended an open invitation to the entire country to participate in a number of 'political laboratories'.

These labs would effectively function as a platform for crowd-sourcing the party's political programme. The commentators didn't know whether to cry or laugh. Most of them settled on a perception of The Alternative as a sort of practical joke, or at best a protest party. None of them predicted any real likelihood that Uffe and his colleagues would get enough votes to even get a single seat in the parliament.

Once again the establishment had underestimated Uffe Elbæk. At the parliamentary election on 18 June 2014, The Alternative got almost 5 per cent of the votes, earning as many as nine seats. Among all the Danish politicians Uffe came in at number ten on the number of personal votes.

What the commentators hadn't understood was that even the rules of politics could be innovated and improved upon. Whilst the experts weren't really curious about The Alternative, the voters were. Crowdsourcing a party programme might not have been done before, but that doesn't mean it's impossible.

With its six core values – courage, generosity, transparency, humility, humour and empathy – The Alternative is indeed setting the tone for something new, fresh and unconventional. Humour is not exactly what comes to mind for most of us when thinking of politics (mockery and sarcasm excluded). And how often does a politician strike us as being humble?

Whilst curiosity is without a doubt awesome, it has a shadow side that we need to address as well. When we are very curious, there is a risk that we will often be distracted. When I tell people I have started ten businesses (during a fifteen-year period) they might think that I am bragging, but in fact

I am admitting a weakness. I can now see that it would have been better if I could have started fewer initiatives and given each of them more focus and patience – but my curiosity has seduced me quite a few times. I have written books, started a school in India, launched a new kind of book-publishing company for the American market, created an on-line donation platform for charities, fought hard to buy a chain of shops selling health-food products, and much more. Clearly my curiosity hasn't only been an asset, it's often been a liability too.

Focus is important. Curiosity is essential. So what we need is *focussed curiosity*. For instance, when we are on a mission to grow, say, an e-commerce company selling home-decor products, it's really useful to be curious about interior design trends, industry benchmarks for average order size and conversion rates, what makes our customers happy, how they are using our products, etc. It is less helpful to be captivated by a device for the shipping industry, or obsessed with whether we have what it takes to write a fantasy novel. All is good stuff, but in its right time. For our leadership to be effective we need clarity of direction, purpose and vision. Otherwise, it becomes very difficult for others to follow our lead.

Practice

Have a conversation with someone you normally wouldn't talk to. Someone that you have judged to be very different from you. Be curious if the other person knows something you don't.

Read a book whose premise you strongly disagree with. Be intentional about learning three new facts.

When you notice yourself being curious about something that is not related to the goals or the vision you have set for yourself, ask yourself if this is: a) a distraction, b) a call for a deliberate change of course, or c) a previously unseen angle for how best to move ahead on your priorities. Use your curiosity; don't get used by it.

4. Infuse Your Leadership with 'Ecosophy'

As he declared war on Nazi Germany, the celebrated British Prime Minister Winston Churchill began planning his butterfly house in Chartwell, Kent. A distraction from the difficult job ahead, or a much-needed reminder of nature's ultimate symbol of transformation and freedom? This only Churchill knew. Suffice it to say that from a young age he loved spending time in nature. Fascinated by watching caterpillars transform into beautiful butterflies, he relished seeing them take their maiden flight. I randomly found this endearing passage written by a young Winston to his mother, when I was distracting myself in the library at the beautiful Ashridge House, the home of our academic partner for this book.

'I never have done work in my holidays and I will not begin now. It will be very good if this is not forced upon me,' writes a thirteen-year-old Winston in a letter to his mother, pleading with her not to assign him any work during his holidays. He continues, 'I am never at a loss for anything to do whilst I'm in the country, for I shall be occupied with "butterflying" all day.'[1]

Yes, butterflying was that important to Winston. Could this have been the secret to his ability to keep calm and carry on?

You may wonder why we are discussing nature in a book about how to be a leader. We feel strongly that the blinkers must come off. Nature *is* an important stakeholder for next-generation leaders. This point must be lived and experienced, not merely understood conceptually. As a stakeholder in your leadership practice, nature will move you, nurture you, break your heart open and teach you. But only if you let her.

Here is a gem of wisdom I recently received from an elder in the Tejakula village in northern Bali. He teaches the leaders in his community to master three relationships. The human-to-human relationship, which requires an open heart and the removal of the notion of separation. The human-to-the-divine relationship, which is very much alive in Bali, known as 'the land of a thousand temples'. And the human-to-nature relationship, which also posits the removal of separation, seeing nature not as something 'out there' and something to be afraid of, but rather as an organism we are a part of.

Chris Nichols, co-director of the Ashridge Masters in Sustainability and Responsibility programme, and his team help their students cultivate 'a deeper appreciation of nature as "we", a living system which we need to engage with, because we are one. This is not a moral position, it's a scientific appreciation that if a subsystem (humans) harms a higher-level system (nature) we will not thrive. A subsystem cannot thrive without the higher-order system on which it depends.' He passionately believes that the world needs leaders with 'ecosophy', a term coined by Norwegian philosopher Arne Naess, representing a dynamic and evolving sense of the wisdom required to live in harmony with the earth.

You might object that the practice of observing and appreciating nature is not new. Indeed Mother Nature has captured our imagination for thousands of years. She has been an inspiration for art, design, music, literature. Take, for example, Antoni Gaudí, whose juvenile arthritis contributed to his solitary tendencies and close connection with nature. Unable to play with other children, he spent his time alone, observing animals, plants and stones. One of the most famous architects of his time, Gaudí went on to create work that is intensely organic, full of imagery from nature and religion, earning him the nickname 'God's architect'.

For Gaudí, nature was more than just decoration. His structures emulate both aesthetic and functional benefits found in nature – arches mirroring ribcages, columns mirroring trees or human bones, roof structures mirroring leaves. Following nature's blueprint, Gaudí was not only able to reduce the materials required for his structures, but he also managed to transform Barcelona into an art gallery celebrating the beauty, wisdom and joyful expression of nature.

Along the way, however, it seems that we got caught in the notion that we, as humans at the top of the food chain, know best. And we began seeing nature as 'other'. An unfortunate consequence of this is that we have developed a tendency to exploit it.

Next-generation leadership therefore needs to be framed from a position of oneness with nature. And this starts by having a 'deep experience', like the one Joseph Jaworski describes in *Presence: Exploring Profound Change in People, Organizations and Society*.

It happened in Baja California, Mexico, whilst

Joseph was participating in a 'Sacred Passage' vision quest. On the last day of the seven days he spent in solitude by the beach, Joseph describes this encounter:

I became aware of another presence and glanced to my left, where, just fifteen feet away on another of the boulders, was a female sea lion . . . She didn't move, just looked at me peacefully with huge, soft brown eyes. We stayed there, relaxing in each other's presence for several minutes. Then she began to move, and I thought she was leaving – but I was wrong. She climbed off the rock and came toward me, stopping only eight or ten feet away. She rested her head between two rocks that formed a V-shape, as if to mimic my chin resting on my staff. She rubbed her cheeks against one rock and then the other. Finally she gave a big yawn and then just sat there looking into my eyes. Her eyes were beautiful, kind – and sorrowful, I thought. She stayed maybe ten minutes with me then very gently moved away from the rocks and made her way back to the ocean. At that very moment the entire sky turned red – not just the western sky but the entire sky, all of it, from east to west. I don't think I've ever seen this happen before, and I just stood there, overcome, moved to the depths of my whole being.[2]

Joseph later affirmed that back there on that beach 'nature had become my teacher. She had helped me access who I am and what my work really is.'[3]

To understand what happened during this encounter, let's apply a framework offered by Erich Jantsch. The Austrian-born astrophysicist and systems theorist outlined three distinct levels of human knowledge: the rational, the mythical and the evolutionary. Imagine life as if it were water flowing in a riverbed. Imagine yourself sitting by the side of the river. You observe the water-flow, the vegetation around the riverbank, you measure the water's rise and fall, its temperature. This is the rational system of knowing, and the relationship between the observer and the observed is that of 'I' and 'it'. If Joseph had just observed the sea lion for a few minutes, not connecting with the creature, this would have been his experience of the encounter.

If by chance, as you observe the river, you fall in, you now have a different type of knowledge –

knowledge by experience. You are now immersed in that which you seek to know. This plunges you into the mythical system of knowledge. If you embrace this mythical system and choose to remain in the river for a while, you no longer view your relationship with the river as 'I' and 'it' but as 'I' and 'thou'. Joseph had been in this remote part of Mexico for nearly fourteen days, seven of which were spent in complete solitude. With no distractions, no contact with the world, focussing only on practices that were meant to connect him with nature, he experienced a wordless dialogue with the sea lion, and a soul-to-soul way of relating.

By merging with the river, and learning to swim until it becomes a glorious free-flowing dance, you enter the third level of knowledge, the evolutionary system. At this point 'I' and 'thou' become 'we'. The intense presence of the sea lion and the connection Joseph felt with her created an opening for a profound transformation of his spirit and his mind, which allowed him to feel for a moment one with the whole of nature and everything there is.

Chris Nichols describes this type of experience as 'a moment that touches us and, with a gasp, allows us to see and feel the intricate marvel of the web of life of which we are a part'.

The natural world can provide both perspective and comfort.

It's easy to think that these insights are nothing but distant visions, disconnected from our leadership, if our work has us spending most of our time in an office, in concrete jungles. Still, as Chris Nichols reminds us, we must hold the awareness that we humans form a subsystem which is part of – and greatly depends on – a higher-level system: Mother Nature. Infusing your leadership with ecosophy – the wisdom required to live in harmony with the earth – ensures that the decisions you make as a leader will not exploit one of our most important stakeholders.

May your leadership come from a place of oneness with nature.

Practice

I hope by now you are open to seeing nature's playground as a great catalyst for clarity, wisdom and creativity. When faced with important decisions, or looking for new solutions, spend one day 'butterflying' like Winston, observing and appreciating nature. Then ask yourself: *What would nature do?*

For those ready to have a more profound experience, we suggest spending a full day doing a Deep Time Walk on the coast of Dartmoor in the UK.

Created by Dr Stephan Harding, resident ecologist at Schumacher College, the walk involves walking slowly for 4.5 kilometres, each kilometre representing 1 billion years of earth history. Experiencing history on this scale is deeply transformational.[4]

II. You + Others

Leaders constantly have to inspire and enlist others in their cause, and as such leadership is an ongoing and multifaceted conversation. In Chapter 5 we look at what we can learn about communication from the Clipper Round the World Yacht Race, where twelve yachts filled with amateurs set sail for a year at sea. We explore how leaders can ensure that they know what is going on right under their nose, and how conflicts and misunderstandings can be resolved with a method from Native American culture.

When groups or teams come together, whether in an organization, a movement or a community, a heartbeat emerges. In Chapter 6 we explore the notion of culture and bring you stories of leaders that have managed to create organizational cultures in which people thrive, and the stunning results they achieved.

Traditionally, we have thought of leadership as a lonely post. With the emergence of ever-increasing

When the going gets tough, communication is key.

complexity in the way organizations function, we need to retire this perspective and replace it with a dedication to joint decision-making and true co-creation. At Rainmaking we have chosen this path, and in Chapter 7 we share what this approach has taught us since our start in 2006.

We all know that we should ideally give before we take, but sometimes we can lack a deep enough motivation to carry out the good intentions. In Chapter 8 we share a very personal story of altruism, to illustrate how we all have the opportunity and capacity to show up as a leader in someone's life.

5. Master the Art of Communication

On 22 April 1969, when Robin Knox-Johnston returned on his boat *Suhaili* to Falmouth, England, a new life began for the thirty-year-old sailor. As the winner of the high-profile *Sunday Times* Golden Globe Race, Robin had the honour of being the first man in the world to perform a single-handed non-stop circumnavigation of the globe. The journey took him more than ten months, and was no small feat. One of his competitors, Donald Crowhurst, committed suicide during the long isolation. And Knox-Johnston, by no means a wealthy man at the time, generously donated his prize money to Donald's widow and children.

Robin Knox-Johnston was awarded a CBE in 1969, and knighted in 1995 – the year before he launched Clipper Ventures, which has since made it possible for amateur crew members to follow in his footsteps and make the journey all the way around our blue planet.

Clipper Round the World Yacht Race is an

extreme sport in its own league. Anyone above the age of eighteen can sign up. The trip takes a full year and offers its participants radical experiences most of us can hardly imagine. Participants can expect epic Southern Ocean storms, the mountainous seas of the North Pacific, long stretches of very limited sleep, no privacy at all – and lifelong memories.

Designed as a race, the event consists of twelve Clipper Race yachts. Each yacht has an experienced skipper and a crew of fifteen to twenty 'civilians' ranging from taxi drivers, investment bankers and housewives to engineers, students and rugby players.

Lifelong memories for sure, but maybe more than that? Ashridge Business School eyed an opportunity to go behind the scenes to investigate what we can all learn about leadership from what happens on those yachts during the Clipper Race. The researchers were curious to know if there was a winning formula, and how a skipper would ideally think and act to keep his amateur crew safe and thriving under these harsh conditions.

The report came out in 2013 and made it clear that communication was the underpinning success factor for those long stretches of time on the ocean.[1] The yachts are identical, the skippers are all experts in their craft, and the route is easy enough to calculate. What makes all the difference is how the skipper communicates with his team. It doesn't only determine who wins the race, but also defines what kind of experience both the crew and the skipper will have during that year at sea.

In a way, this should come as no surprise. We all know that every time people get together communication happens – verbal as well as nonverbal. We probably remember plenty of examples from our own families as well as our workplaces where communication broke down, which made progress impossible. We humans misunderstand each other so easily.

Still, one could argue that sailing a yacht is a very specific task, and that in a storm there cannot be room for being sensitive about how people talk to each other – so under these circumstances more hardcore measurements like muscle power, sailing track-record, resilience and endurance would outweigh communication as the defining factors. But no, communication ruled again – and is to a large extent what creates and activates the other strengths. A yacht with a skipper who knew how to communicate well with his crew would as a consequence get a more resilient, agile and capable team. These insights can serve as a welcome reminder that in any kind of leadership communication is really the backbone to everything we do.

Here are the five distinctive skills which we believe are key for effective leadership:

1. Inspiring, storytelling, enlisting and selling.
2. Understanding what others are saying.
3. Resolving conflicts and misunderstandings.
4. Being open and transparent, including about the difficult stuff.
5. Creating a space where others will feel safe to tell you the truth.

We can get by as leaders without mastering all five skills, but there's a massive opportunity if we can get our ducks in a row here.

To become a leader who is both an evangelist and a storyteller is the most talked-about and obvious communication aspiration, so chances are that you have already read quite a few books on the topic. You have learnt about presentation techniques, pitching, influencing strategies and good salesmanship. You have probably heard the argument that in business everything is selling; a leader will constantly sell the vision, the company and the products to his investors, employees, customers and other stakeholders.

Important as this skill-set is, it is hardly overlooked in leadership literature, so let's move on to
the second type of communication: the leader as a
listener, and the leader's ability to exchange viewpoints and foster mutual understanding.

This part is really difficult for many of us – and
chances are that the more people we are leading the
worse at it we gradually become. Why? Because
with many people to lead there will be more potential conversations to be had than we can ever cope
with. Ideally we should be genuinely talking to everyone in our organization every day, but as soon
as the organization has a dozen members or more,
that becomes impossible. Busyness sets in, which
means that the leader has to gauge, every waking
minute, whether this or that discussion or meeting
is worth the time.

Megan Reitz, Director at Ashridge Business
School, has researched the topic extensively and au-
thored the book *Dialogue in Organizations*. In our
interview Megan explains that leaders very often
find themselves in dialogues with their employees
where they have a parallel thought process running: 'Is this conversation worth having?' Of course,
when this happens, most conversation partners
will sense that they are not fully appreciated and
pull back.

As leaders we can fool ourselves into thinking that our approach is effective; we keep conversations very short, and only a few of our team members 'disturb' us. The cliché of 'my door is always open' can be used to guard us against critique, and it's easy enough to signal our reservations and impatience in subtle yet very effective ways: a distant glance, quick repeated nods, a look at the watch, a reserved smile. We are very busy, and soon enough we will only hear what we want to hear, and we won't have a clue about what is really going on in people's heads.

To what extent do you feel that your leader truly understands your perspective, viewpoints and ideas for improvements? How about the people you are leading? Do you know what's on their minds, what is keeping them awake at night, what they think could be done to improve your organization's performance?

It's easy to shut down communication. It's much harder to foster genuine conversations that lead to mutual understanding and powerful knowledge-sharing.

My partners and I were fortunate to discover Professor Stephen R. Covey's *The 7 Habits of Highly Effective People* the same year we started Rainmaking. We all got very excited about Covey's simple yet incredibly powerful framework. Especially the principle of 'seek first to understand, then to be understood'. Covey explained how things go awry when multiple parties in a conversation try to get their point of view across simultaneously. Yet, that is what normally happens – particularly in organizational settings where time is scarce and we want to be productive and efficient. We listen mainly for a pause so we can jump in and offer our own perspective on the matter. This is not a real conversation. The Native Americans knew that, and they used a 'talking stick' to cope with the human tendency to be predominantly occupied with our own thoughts and beliefs. And it's a great tool for resolving conflicts and misunderstandings.

American philosopher and professor of business ethics at the University of Virginia, R. Ed Freeman encourages his students and clients to use conflict and polarity – defined as 'interdependent opposites'[2] – as a way to create more value. He calls this 'constructive conflict' and it begins with understanding the conflicting perspectives as well as their inherent tensions.

The way the talking stick works is that only the person who holds it is allowed to speak. The listeners have to be quiet and attentive, not show-ing any signs of impatience or disapproval. Only when the person talking has nothing more to say on the matter does the stick get passed on. The method assures that everyone is heard, and no one gets interrupted, intimidated or ignored.

Professor Covey added an important dimension to make the method suitable to resolve difficult con-flicts: When you have listened to the person with the talking stick, you should be able to repeat what the person just told you. That might sound easy enough, but the hard part is that the person who has been speaking has to agree that you have un-derstood the message. If there is severe disagree-ment in the air, you can be sure that you won't succeed in the first attempt. You will hear 'No, no, that's not what I mean' quite a few times before you get it right.

What's so magical about this approach is that the moment we internalize that success is to truly understand what is being communicated to us, we completely shift our focus and start to really listen. Where our competitive nature previously prompted us to focus on getting our own message across, we now work hard to be successful in understanding the other person – which is a striking difference!

Of course much more could be said on the topic

of understanding what others are actually saying, and resolving disagreements and conflicts. But, if you internalize this simple yet powerful lesson – seek first to understand, then to be understood – it will work wonders for your communication skills as a leader.

Let's now move on to the third skill: being open and transparent, especially about the difficult stuff. Whilst that might sound easy enough – 'just be honest' – in fact it's wildly controversial and miles away from what happens in most organizations to-day, whether we are talking about start-ups, corporates, NGOs or government offices.

Let's begin with start-ups. How many founders do you think dare to be open with their team about funding running out, let alone sharing the bad news with their investors? One common misconception is that as founders we should always be up-beat, and when people ask how it's going with our start-up the only right answer is different variations of 'awesome'.

There is one big problem with this conventional wisdom. It assumes that team members and investors are stupid or naive – which is obviously not the case. The fact is that we cannot fool anyone, so we might as well stop trying. Trust is immediately eradicated when people sense we are not being honest with them. They might not know exactly where the fire is, but they will notice the smoke. None of us enjoys being kept in the dark, and the result is a quick drop in morale.

I know from first-hand experience that as long as we do our best, and are completely honest and respectful, discussing difficult topics with our stakeholders will only strengthen the relationships. Around half of the businesses I have started during the last ten years eventually had to be closed down, with people getting fired and investors losing money. Still, team members and investors kept believing in me, often accepting jobs and investing new money in my next venture. They knew that there were no bad intentions, that we all worked hard on something worthwhile, and that everyone was given full information – especially when things went awry.

My teams have always had full access to our books. It's a lot easier to get everyone to fight for profitability when they know the budget and understand the P&L statement. It's valid to be concerned that morale might be hurt when funding is running out, and people start to worry about their jobs. The founders shouldn't sit at their desks and cry about what is a natural state for a start-up, but rather be out talking to investors, and be a hopeful voice in the team. Everyone knows that a start-up can sink. It's worse to be on the ship if the captain is trying to cover up the fact that we are taking in water, than if he's out there on the deck, telling everyone what is going on, and taking the lead in fixing the problem.

This principle doesn't only apply in start-ups. Chip Conley had been the founder and CEO of his chain of hotels, Joie de Vivre Hotels, for twenty-one years. In 2008, as the financial crisis got really bad, the timing for expansion plans at his company could hardly have been worse. After prudently building his business for years, Chip had started a very rapid expansion, opening fifteen new hotels within less than two years. He now had 3,500 employees and a huge cost base in an industry that has proven to be particularly exposed to economic downturn.

Chip vividly remembers an occasion in November 2008 where he was going on stage in front of the top eighty managers in his organization. A few days earlier two of his colleagues on the executive board had encouraged him to deliver a speech that could cheer up the managers – to find a way to make them happy again. 'At that time I could see that the sense of despair in my company was enormous,' Chip recalls.

He did write the cheerleading speech. But five minutes before he was going to deliver it, he instead handed the piece of paper to his executive colleague by his side, asking her to 'please hold on to this speech, I might use it later, but I won't use it today'. Chip felt awful about the situation they were in, and his gut instinct told him to be honest rather than phony.

Three months earlier, Chip had had a heart attack culminating in a flatline experience. Or rather nine of them during a period of ninety minutes, according to his doctors. With a newly gained sense of perspective Chip wasn't afraid to be vulnerable any more. So he went up in front of his eighty managers and much to everyone's surprise started off by saying: '2009 is going to be an awful year . . .' Chip explained how they had got themselves in trouble, and admitted that he didn't yet know what the solution would be. He talked about his flatline experience that had so far been kept a secret. And he called out the elephants in the room: fear and anxiety.

'Instead of giving people sugar or coffee as a fix, I talked about how we could create meaning together. How we needed to figure this one out as a team,' Chip tells us in our interview. The message Chip sent was that it was okay to be vulnerable.

That in this company truth was welcome, even when it wasn't particularly cheerful. Chip showed trust in his colleagues. He talked about how even in the middle of all this he still felt confident that, with all the great people in their organization, they would find a way to pull through together. And they did. In June 2010 the business had been turned around, and after twenty-four years, Chip sold Joie de Vivre Hotels and moved on to new adventures. Today, looking back, Chip has no doubt that being honest that day in November 2008 was the right choice, and it became a turning point for the atmosphere and culture of the organization.

Transparency and openness go both ways, and it's an equally important leadership responsibility to get the people you are leading to feel safe enough to be brutally honest with you.

In the autumn of 2015, VW was all over the news with their 'Diesel-gate' scandal, a sustained and sophisticated software scam with the purpose of making their engines unlawfully pass environmental tests. After a long and glorious career, VW Chairman and CEO, Martin Winterkorn, was forced to step down in shame. Just a year after Forbes named Winterkorn the fifty-eighth most powerful person in the world, the sixty-eight-year-old engineer, doctor and PhD has fallen from the stars, and can look forward to criminal investigations for years to come. Not exactly the legacy and retirement he was dreaming of. Before the scandal he looked poised to succeed in his ambition to make VW the biggest car manufacturer in the world. Now instead VW's stock has plummeted, and millions of cars are going back to the factories to be rectified. Some even predict that the whole of Germany's image for quality and credibility will be strongly damaged by this unscrupulous deception.

Martin Winterkorn claims that he didn't have any knowledge of the extensive fraud that was going on right under his nose. To which commentators, experts and media have responded that if that is the case, then the CEO hasn't been doing his job properly. A CEO should know what goes on in his or her company. In many countries the legislation underlines this principle; for instance, a legal guide for CEOs in the United States from Chief Executive Research explains: 'It is critical to understand that the CEO need not have actual knowledge of or participation in the criminal activity – just having the authority to exercise control over the situation that led to the criminal violation is enough.'[3]

How do we as leaders allow for bad news to reach us? It starts with us realizing that, when it comes to communication flow, as leaders we are on the edge of the organization rather than inside of it. Megan Reitz tells of a leader she was coaching who had the goal of becoming Managing Director of his business. He did achieve his goal, but was surprised to find that just two hours after his promotion was announced all his friends in the organization, who used to come by and chat, found new places in the office to hang out.

Megan explains: 'In many ways the leader knows the least of what is really going on in the organization. For the employees there will always be a sense of jeopardy in sharing information with a person that holds power over their careers.' According to Megan, as leaders we need to be really good at levelling with our colleagues, creating the space for them to feel safe, so they can openly express their concerns and opinions to us.

It's one thing to create this atmosphere in a conversation; it's quite another to show that you honour that trust in your subsequent actions. If telling the truth turns out to be a terrible mistake, then rest assured that in the future you will be – like Martin Winterkorn claims to have been – the last to know.

Only by remaining humble, curious and acting with the utmost integrity can we as leaders create an environment that invites our colleagues to speak their truth.

Practice

The next time you are dealing with conflict or disagreement try the principle of 'seek first to understand, then to be understood'.

Think of someone in your organization with whom you normally do not go beyond small talk. Make it your mission to have a conversation where you learn at least three new things that can be used to improve your organization's performance.

Practise your ability to be open and transparent. When you sense that someone could benefit from a piece of information you have, share it instead of holding on to it. Have faith that you won't lose anything by doing so.

6. Define your Riverbanks

No discussion about leadership would be sound without addressing the question of culture. Intuitively we know it – whether we work in corporate America or a start-up in Delhi. Whenever people come together in groups or organizations, a heartbeat emerges.

But what is culture, how can we create it, and – more importantly – how can we evolve it?

Culture is really a deceptively simple concept. Whenever people come together, culture happens. It's inevitable. Like cells in an organism, colliding, hooking together and breaking apart in an endless process of creation and destruction, we bring culture about moment by moment. There's no escape from this process. And the longer we swim in a certain culture, good or bad, the more we begin to internalize it and create more of it. As such, culture is dynamic and alive. This means that it can be shifted, evolved, and of course, intentionally created. But it takes conscious leadership for this to happen.

As organizational culture is more complex and challenging to create, we'll look at culture in the corporate context. However, the same principles apply to our social settings and all other ways in which we come together as human beings.

With the caveat that no company is perfect, and all leaders are on a continuum, learning and evolving, in the following paragraphs we'll look at how two leaders have managed to create extraordinary organizations. Both companies operate in very tough markets – retail and hospitality – arguably the hardest industries in which to create cultures focussed on making employees happy. These two leaders have made culture and people their competitive advantage. So let's take a look.

In the spring of 2005, with the doors firmly closed on the six-year relationship with my college sweetheart, ink barely dry on our divorce decree, I began to search for a new home. In addition to the psychological stress of going through this transition, I also found myself with quite a practical challenge. How would I fit everything into my new, and significantly smaller home? Then one day a friend took me to The Container Store on Wisconsin Avenue in Washington DC. I still remember how I felt, walking into the spacious, airy store which seemed to have everything one might need to put even the most chaotic of lives in order. The staff were friendly and helpful, and the products were delightful. I realize this may be an odd thing to say about storage and organization products, but, at that time in my life, discovering The Container Store was really exciting. I later learnt that my experience in the store that day was the outcome of an intentionally and lovingly architected corporate culture.

Founded in 1978 with a mission to 'help people organize and simplify their lives', The Container Store has since been providing order in our ever-more chaotic modern world, and has become something of a poster child for employee-centric organizations in the US. How and why did they do this?

One manifestation of this philosophy was the idea to rename Valentine's Day 'We Love Our Employees Day'. On this day, the company's leadership brings chocolates and gifts and tells their employees that they are loved. But they also put their money where their mouth is: they pay their employees dramatically more than any of their competitors – think average annual salaries of nearly $50,000 compared to a retail-industry average of

$24,000 in 2013.[1] If you know anything about the retail industry, especially the US retail industry, you will agree that this is pretty remarkable.

However, as we all know, whilst money is an important motivator, it's not *the* most important. In his TED talk 'The Power of Motivation', bestselling author Daniel Pink outlines three intrinsic motivators: autonomy, mastery and purpose. Somehow, attuned to our intrinsic need to be really good at what we do, the folks behind The Container Store have always invested in training their employees. They spend more than 260 hours training full-time employees on topics such as leadership, operational skills, product knowledge, space design, etc. All important lessons to ensure their people achieve a level of mastery and comfort in their work. In the process, of course, their employees become more invested in the company and stay longer, some even for their entire careers. The employee-turnover rate in the US retail industry is on average 100 per cent, meaning that an employee only stays one year with the company on average. At The Container Store, that number is only 10 per cent. With this ethos, it should come as no surprise that this company has been on *Fortune*'s 100 Best Companies to Work For list for fifteen years. Remember, we're talking about retail.

You might argue that this fanatical emphasis on caring for employees can only be achieved in smaller companies, where the leader can bring his or her presence and vision to the workplace every day. And there is of course something to that argument. It's much easier to keep your vision and purpose alive and permeating your organization when you can be there every day in the trenches with your employees. But caring for their employees didn't cease to be important to The Container Store's management as the company grew. Quite the opposite: it became even more vital to find a way to 'scale' the culture they had created in the early days. With seventy stores in twenty-six US states, and 6,000 employees, it's easy to see why we are inspired by The Container Store and their CEO, Kip Tindell's, leadership.

Today, boxes from their original collection are on permanent display at the Museum of Modern Art. Their headquarters, attached to a 1.1 million square foot warehouse, sit proudly across the street from an Amazon.com warehouse in an industrial area near Dallas/Fort Worth International Airport. But the beginnings were far more humble. A fan of organizing things from a young age, Kip Tindell launched the company together with Garrett Boone, his supervisor from his first retail job selling paint

at a Montgomery Wards store. From the very beginning they had been intent on hiring people who
would enjoy working together, paying them well,
and being transparent about the company's fi-
nances with their employees. 'We're selling empty
boxes,' says Kip in a *Bloomberg* interview. 'We need
a better-educated, motivated and trained employee
to get a customer to buy twelve items to organize
that toy area instead of just one.'[2]

We asked Kip to share some stories that inspired
him to be the leader he is today.

'More than forty years ago, I heard Herb Kelle-
her, the legendary co-founder of Southwest Air-
lines, say "A company is stronger if it is bound by
love rather than by fear." When I heard that, I was
completely taken by it. I knew instinctively that
this is how I wanted to lead my own company,' Kip
recalls.

Kip and his co-founders went on to create a business built on this vision that a company is stronger if bound by love rather than fear. A company
with a culture intently focussed on taking care of
their employees and making sure that everyone as-
sociated with their organization thrives.

Kip truly believes that what they are doing at
The Container Store changes lives. Not only the
lives of their employees but also of other stake-

holder groups such as customers, suppliers and the wider community. The management's purpose sounds more like a calling. 'There's a Zen quality to being organized,' Kip often says. And what he found along the way was that not making profit their number-one priority actually made the company more profitable.

You may not see it, but you can sense their culture when you walk through their doors.

It is this certain *je ne sais quoi*, this intangible something, that Danny Meyer's restaurants have in spades.

Born and raised in St Louis, Missouri, Danny Meyer grew up in a family that provided the nourishing environment in which his passion for food developed. His father's extensive travels exposed Danny to different cultures, types of cuisine and ways of life. He gained his first experience in the restaurant business as an assistant manager at Pesca, an Italian restaurant in New York City, which inspired him to undertake culinary studies in Italy and France. He opened his first restaurant, Union Square Cafe, in 1985, at the age of twenty-seven. It took nine years of dedication towards mastering his business before opening his second restaurant, Gramercy Tavern.

He's always believed that the role of a restaurant

is more than just putting good food on the plate. 'It's also to make sure people are a little happier when they leave than when they came in,' says Danny.

When asked about his first year as a restaurateur in a competitive market like New York City, Danny says, 'Nothing mattered more than surrounding myself with a great team and pleasing our guests. My entire first year was trying to prove that a team of nice people trying to please their customers was the recipe for restaurant success.'

Fast-forward to today. Danny's company, Union Square Hospitality Group (USHG), runs eleven restaurants, including five of the top-twenty-rated restaurants in New York City. His restaurants and chefs have earned twenty-five James Beard Awards, and some of his restaurants have multiple Michelin stars.

But it wasn't the awards that caught the attention of a bright NYU Stern School of Business PhD student. Susan Reilly Salgado's twenty-year relationship with USHG began as a guest at Danny's first restaurant, Union Square Cafe. Fascinated by the culture and hospitality she experienced as a guest, she convinced Danny to allow her to conduct her dissertation research on USHG's organizational culture. She later joined the company in 2003 as its first Director of Culture and Learning, and in 2010, together with Danny, she launched Hospitality Quotient, the learning and consulting arm of USHG.

In her research, Susan has learnt that Danny hires according to what he calls a 'hospitality quotient', a set of psychological traits, including optimistic warmth, insatiable curiosity to learn, a strong work ethic, empathy, self-awareness and integrity. He then ensures that employees have all the skills training they need in order to master their work. Only then are they able to manifest this set of wonderful personality traits, their 'hospitality quotient'.

We asked Susan to help us understand this intangible concept of organizational culture. 'Culture is a shared system of values, beliefs, norms and accepted behaviours. The sharing part is the most critical element. When leaders don't define a culture, the group will define it with the values, beliefs and behaviours they are willing to tolerate from each other,' she explains.

Metaphors are a great way to reflect on business phenomena, giving us a degree of perspective. Susan tells us that the metaphor most commonly used at USHG to help new managers understand the notion of culture is the river. Imagine the water in a river representing the people that are part of your organization. There's plenty of room for everyone to swim around freely, to be creative and express their unique selves. But the water all flows in one direction and shouldn't flow over the riverbanks. The boundaries of culture are represented by the riverbanks.

Let's put this in a broader context. If we follow the river's ebb and flow we'll see that all rivers eventually surrender their waters into a sea or an ocean. Similarly, the culture we create in our organizations flows into the wider body of our economic and social landscapes. As such, the culture you create in your organization matters, not just to your employees and stakeholders. It makes for a better society, and a better world.

This is a lesson every leader and every *aspiring* leader should take note of.

Practice
Whether or not you are the leader of the organization where you spend your working hours, take the time to identify and connect with its heartbeat.

Pay attention. Then consider the fo
ing questions:

- How does it feel to walk into work each day, especially on Monday morning?
- Are there behaviours that don't serve the highest good of the people working in your organization?
- How would you design the culture in your organization?
- What kind of behaviours would you like to foster?

As a leader, shaping your company's culture – defining your riverbanks – is going to be one of your most important tasks. Start with a simple yet powerful practice like one of the culture-shaping practices common at Whole Foods Market.

Co-CEOs John Mackey and Walter Robb aim to foster a culture of appreciation in their company. They believe that giving as well as receiving appreciation has the power to shift consciousness. So at the end of all meetings, they've set aside time for 'voluntary appreciation'.

'By ending meetings with appreciation, we can shift people out of their space of judgment and back into one of love,' says John Mackey.[3]

Sounds too simple? Give it a go, and behold the power of a group of people banding together, bringing to life the purpose and values of your organization.

7. Decision-making is a Team Sport

Can a company be run by six co-CEOs? Before you answer, hear this:

When we started Rainmaking back in 2006, none of us founders felt like any one should be more in charge than the rest. For a decade now we have been co-creating, and making every important decision collectively. That might sound inefficient and hippieish to you, but take one look at the six of us, and I think you will agree that we are neither. The trick is to notice who is the natural leader in any given situation, and seamlessly switch – sometimes within minutes – between being a leader and being a follower.

One of us is a numbers wizard, thus he naturally takes the lead when we make budgets, financial reports, and talk about which business models make the most sense.

Another one of my co-founders is the techie among us, so when we are building an algorithm to extract information from thousands of websites and present it neatly to the user, he is calling the shots.

When making strategic decisions for our business, we talk it all through, and we use our combined experience and intelligence to analyse pros and cons, working our way to a joint decision. Not once has it been necessary to vote. We have always managed to arrive at a conclusion that all of us feel comfortable with.

Call it collective leadership, distributed decision power, situational leadership or something else. You get the point.

Though uncontroversial to us, the choice not to have just one CEO has puzzled, and even upset, many of those we have met along the way. Traditional thinking, it seems, is that any organization, be it a company, a non-profit, a city or a country, needs to have one person – and only one person – that is ultimately in charge. A ship can only have one captain, right? The arguments people use to explain that age-old conviction go something like this:

- If there is more than one captain, they will start arguing about how to weather a storm, what time to set sail in the morning, and how to treat a disobedient crew member. It will be chaos!

- With more captains how will the crew know who to ask for instructions, and which orders to follow? It's necessary to have a clear chain of command.

- A good captain knows how best to involve his team, and when to ask for input, thus there is no need for more than one person at the top.

Whilst these are valid arguments they are not the only truth. People today are much more aware, collaborative and educated than when the 'one ship, one captain' rule became the norm. Here are the three key advantages we have harvested from our unusual mode of practice:

1. Better decisions

We believe that the decisions you make in negotiation with a group of equals are better than those made by any one person. Yes, a single CEO will hopefully listen to input before arriving at a conclusion, but in the absence of a formal hierarchy there is a greater chance that all focus is on the strength of the arguments, and not on who is making them.

2. More commitment

When we have made a decision, and go out into the world to implement it, we do so with authentic commitment. It's our own decision, not something imposed upon us. Do you remember a situation where you didn't agree with the orders you needed to carry out? How did that make you feel, and did you honestly apply all your creativity and commitment to make the solution succeed, or did you half-ass it? I know what I did back when I was captured in a traditional hierarchy.

3. Better team morale

A natural by-product of more distributed authority is better team morale, despite conventional wisdom telling us the opposite. In our case, the six of us stand side by side, and our colleagues really appreciate that. At their former workplaces, far too often they have experienced covert leadership agendas, politics and backstabbing.

It's important to remember that collective or situational leadership is still leadership, and we six cannot just sit around looking bewildered at each other. If no one steps up naturally to take the lead, we need to address this, and make sure there is a dedicated and inspiring leader for every important task and situation. Most often that's not a problem, but sometimes it is. Like with our Rainmaking website. Because we run many businesses we got into the habit of only focussing on the websites for our individual projects, and forgoing the opportunity to tell a compelling and updated story on our parent-company website. None of us took the lead. Only recently did we fix this, which was of course a failure on our part. However, this has more to do with our own learning curve, rather than the collective-leadership model itself.

Our company is small, with around 300 team members, but bigger organizations are embracing new leadership structures as well. Recently, the Amazon-owned online retailer Zappos made headlines with its commitment to becoming a so-called holacracy, a form of organization with no hierarchy and no titles at all. Fourteen per cent of the 1,800-person workforce quit as a result of the radical change, but the founder of Zappos, Tony Hsieh, remains committed to the experiment.

Many of us have probably at some point in our

lives asked ourselves why we really need to have a boss. We might have been frustrated that we couldn't be allowed to make our own decisions. Maybe in the future we all will, at companies like Zappos.

Collective leadership does require a certain structure and discipline to succeed. As a Dane, having my office within a kilometre of Christiania, one of the world's biggest experiments in flat organizing, I am only too aware of how miserably it can fail. Back in the 1970s, a group of free-thinkers, cultural radicals and first-generation hippies snuck under a fence into an abandoned military area. There they started building a state within the state, where normal laws don't apply, where no one pays property taxes, and where all decisions are supposed to be made jointly. Decision-making happens at a weekly gathering in a big warehouse, where everyone, at least in theory, is allowed to present his or her viewpoints freely.

Quickly the result became endless meetings, where ultimately no real decisions were made, and thus an alternative hierarchy formed. This means that today power is shared between a small group of hard-core 'Christianites' and an equally small bunch of drug-dealing criminals, and the place is neither safe, fun nor free-thinking.

Of course, hundreds of people cannot just be expected to show up in a warehouse and be able to make meaningful collective decisions. But it was a nice thought. Today, with technological advances, experiments like Christiania actually have a chance of succeeding. Have you heard of *liquid democracy?*

'Direct' democracy developed in ancient Greece, where 'free men' (women and slaves not invited) would gather at an amphitheatre or on a hillside. There they would listen to talks, debate a matter and eventually all vote on the decision to be made. As our communities, cities and countries grew bigger, this form of direct democracy was no longer viable. Hence we invented the representative democracy.

Today we only rarely have a direct say on a specific political matter. Instead we leave it to the politicians we elect to make the decisions. This often leads to feelings of disempowerment. Also it turns politics into a dysfunctional play of individuals fighting intensely to make themselves look good, and to discredit their rivals. Since we rarely agree on everything with any one candidate, most of us in reality end up picking the one we like the most – and with whom we agree on as many topics as possible. So we vote more on people than on decisions. It's not without reason that Sir Winston Churchill famously said: 'Democracy is the worst form of government, except for all the others.' Now, a new way of governance is emerging, and it might completely change how we lead our societies.

To give you an example of liquid democracy in action:

About a hundred people want to organize a festival together. They don't have any formal leaders; instead, they want to collectively lead the event. However, there are a lot of decisions to be made: which location to choose for the festival, what activities will happen, how many days to stay there, what to eat, etc. Also there is plenty of work to be done, and coordination is necessary. If you were going to the festival, there would probably be some topics that you had a strong opinion on. And other decisions that you were happy to leave to someone else. Not to *anyone* else, but to someone you trusted to be knowledgeable on the matters.

For this festival the participants used software that asked a basic question for each scenario: 'Whom do you trust to make this decision?' The person who got the most votes took charge on the specific matter. It was also possible to vote directly on a decision – and people were encouraged to do that for the matters where they themselves were the person they trusted the most.

If we had a system like this on a national level, I know whom I would trust to make our country's policy on education. And whom I would want to think through our foreign policy. On topics related to entrepreneurship I would vote directly on the decisions – because I feel this is my turf, and I have strong opinions on the matter.

So whilst it might seem crazy for six people to collectively run a business, or for Zappos to have a go at holacracy, in the not-too-distant future, way bigger entities, like cities or countries, might be led much more collaboratively and directly than today.

Just because we have been used to one form of leadership for centuries doesn't mean it is the only way. Rather it might mean that time is ripe for a radical change. We are better together, and we are not *really* together when one person has more stars on his or her shoulders than the rest of us.

It's said to be lonely and cold at the top, but rather than trying to compensate for that by merely taking in the view and installing a bunch of heaters, why not bring more people up there?

Practice

Identify an important decision you have to make in the near future. Who will be good at making this decision together with you – not because of their formal authority but because of their wisdom and competences? Engage them in the decision-making process and trust the outcome to be the right one.

8. Grow Your Appetite for Altruism

One of the few vivid memories I have from my childhood growing up on a sheep farm is of standing in the middle of a great, expansive field, arms stretched out wide, eyes closed, willing myself to be somewhere other than where I was. This was a completely understandable sentiment. Under the leadership of the 'Last Defender of Communism', my country had become, in the words of Ted Koppel, 'a madhouse in which the lunatics were running the asylum and the inmates were punished for their sanity'.[1]

Although I knew very little about the country, the destination for my 'dream travel' was always the United States. I was nine years old, and this practice of willing myself elsewhere was almost a daily ritual.

There wasn't much to support my knowledge and understanding of the place. In Communist Romania the only programming we had on television was one hour of daily propaganda. Electricity would go out by 8 p.m., and our borders were firmly closed. At that age, I didn't know anyone who had ever been to the United States. I suppose I just felt that my life was meant to be more expansive than what that farm could hold.

One day, aged twelve, I informed my mother that I was going to move to the United States. This meant that I needed to learn English. My mother ran an orphanage, so once I had started teaching myself English, I taught the kids at her orphanage what I had learnt.

Three years later, the orphanage received a visit from an American gentleman stationed in Germany. Seth had heard stories about the Romanian orphanages and wanted to help. By that time, my English was just about sufficient to have basic conversations, and I became his interpreter. He created a new charitable foundation, and through this we opened another orphanage, facilitated adoptions overseas and made it possible for children from the orphanage to have access to medical procedures abroad.

Whilst working with Seth I met many interesting people, but the one that has left a deep footprint on my soul is Marylyn Ginsburg. My family and I hosted her in 1995 when she was sent to Romania by her local Rotary Club in Los Angeles to evaluate a potential collaboration to support our orphanage. She was delightful, curious, and took great interest in learning all about our town, the orphanage, and my mother's garden. I remember being quite shocked at how many pictures one person could take.

During the two years working together on Casa Adobe, our orphanage project, I got to learn a lot about Seth's experience, education and worldview. To say that I was impressed by his intelligence and kindness would be an understatement. So when the time came for me to think about higher education, Seth brought me catalogues from two colleges in the United States, encouraging me to apply. With great trepidation I secretly worked on my application to the same college that Seth had attended, saying nothing about it to anyone apart from my mother and my sister. The implications were too important, the outcome too precious to share with the world, so I kept it close to my heart until I had confirmation of the college's decision.

In 1997, the dream I'd had since I was a child came true. I had been accepted to study at the school of my choice – St John's College, a small liberal-arts school in Annapolis, Maryland. Encouraged by Seth, I chose not to dwell on the financial concerns around paying for this education. Anyway,

$125,000 worth of tuition fees was an amount far beyond my comprehension. I took the biggest loan my family had ever seen, of $20,000, which at the time could have bought several houses in my town. And somehow Seth made the rest happen through the foundation.

It wasn't until seventeen years later that I found out where the funding for my education came from.

In 2014 I was in California for a conference and decided to try and reconnect with Marylyn. I hadn't seen her since 1997 when she graciously sent me an airline ticket tucked into a handwritten note inviting me to spend my first Christmas in the US with her and her family out in Los Angeles.

Seventeen years after that Christmas visit, I found myself once again in awe of this woman's kindness and generosity. Marylyn was clearly loved by her family, and her employees, some of whom worked in her businesses until the end of their lives. She is also loved and admired by her community – I learnt that Marylyn had been supporting a wide range of projects in service of her community, the environment, education and the arts.

Over dinner Marylyn casually said, 'I don't believe I told you this before, but I funded a good part of your education, and I'm so proud of the woman you have become.'

Albert Einstein famously wrote: 'The most important decision we make is whether we live in a friendly or a hostile universe.'

At a profound level Marylyn and Seth helped me make my choice, which to this day guides me in everything I do. In my worldview, what I experienced were acts of genuine altruism.

Do you believe in altruism?

If we asked Freud and his followers, they would tell us that human beings show very little inclination to do good. If they happen to nourish altruistic tendencies and behave with kindness, that should not be mistaken for real altruism. They would claim that it's rather a way to suppress aggressive tendencies plaguing the human mind. Indeed, altruism is sometimes defined as 'an outlet for aggressiveness, which instead of being repressed is directed towards "noble" aims'.[2]

But evolutionary scientists suggest that altruism and cooperation have very deep roots in human nature and might in fact have promoted the survival of our species. Darwin, for instance, argued that altruism is an essential part of our social instincts.

In his TED talk, Matthieu Ricard, a researcher,

scientist, Buddhist monk and contemporary advocate of altruism, shows a clip of what he believes to be proof that altruism does indeed exist.[3] A person falls on the train tracks. Just a few seconds before the train whizzes through the station, a man jumps down barely in time to pull the poor fellow to safety. Now, in many claimed cases of altruism, the sceptical mind can object that the good Samaritan was, at the core, acting out of a selfish need to feel good or achieve praise. Watching Matthieu's video, it's difficult to believe there was enough time for such considerations that day at the train station. We probably all know of quite a few instances where selfishness could not have been the motivation for an act of altruism.

If you too are determined to play your role in leading humanity forward then altruism might be the most powerful tool you can reach for. In different forms it's always available to us, regardless of our position in life.

Practice

As a civilization, we have spent centuries thinking that practising altruism is in the province of non-profit or charity work. I still hear people saying, 'Yes, but what difference can one person make?'

As a leader, choose to walk in the light of creative altruism, and inspire others to do the same.

In fact, everything we do begs for a choice to be made. As Martin Luther King put it, we must choose either 'to walk in the light of creative altruism or in the darkness of destructive selfishness'.

Why is this choice so important?

As Matthieu Ricard explains, if we have more consideration for others we will create a more caring economy, more harmony in society and a healthier relationship with the environment. Remarkably, science now shows that practising altruism and compassion brings about structural changes in our brain, and can even change the expression of our genes. How's that for a win-win?

We are all in the same boat, interconnected and interdependent. So, choose altruism, and choose it often, as an individual and as a leader. However small, your acts of altruism will contribute to the evolution of our culture, away from the dominant notion of separation and selfishness to one of cooperation, solidarity and kindness.

III. Shadow

In this part, we examine some shadow-casting monsters like uncertainty, fear, crisis and the ego. The shadow, one of C. G. Jung's most recognizable archetypes, is the part of the unconscious mind which represents weaknesses, shortcomings, irrational instincts – in other words, the unknown 'dark side' of our personality. By definition, it is the part of us that we are least conscious of, and most reluctant to explore.

Sometimes crises hit from out of nowhere. Keep calm and carry on, but how? In Chapter 9 we share how Danish entrepreneur Claus Meyer dealt with a series of crises, when public opinion suddenly turned on him and his business was threatened by a boycott. What Claus learnt during these tough weeks can be useful for all of us, and is a much more profound lesson than it may at first seem.

Uncertainty, and our fear of the natural chaos of

life, can be a wicked force, impacting our leadership. On a deep level, we all know what fear feels like, and that it can make us react in irrational or selfish ways – a far cry from the leaders we want to be. Don't try to 'conquer' or 'beat' fear. Walk with it. Invite it in and be open to what it's here to teach you. Learn from it. In Chapter 10 we show you how one lawyer-turned-entrepreneur-and-author managed to transform uncertainty and fear into fuel for creativity and brilliance.

For some of us, feelings of failure can sneak in – and threaten to destroy us. How do you fail again and again, and still remain strong and dedicated, with the resilience to bounce back? In Chapter 11 we draw on lessons from philosophers as well as American investment companies to offer you some signposts.

A number of researchers have explored the complex relationship between ego and leadership. In Chapter 12, we attempt to demystify the notion of the leader's ego, and invite you to cultivate awareness, in order to develop a more constructive relationship with your ego. For those ready to take the leap, we encourage you to lead from the soul, not the ego.

Bring awareness – in other words, light – into

this part of your work as a leader. The shadow can be a deep source of destructive energy. But, if we develop a more conscious and constructive relationship with our shadow, it can also be a great source of creativity.

9. Leadership During Crisis

On 20 February 2012, Claus Meyer woke up at 6 a.m. in La Paz, Bolivia, where he was working on his recent charity project. Like many of us, Claus has developed the dubious habit of reaching for his phone even before going to the bathroom. A quick look revealed seventy-five new emails, sixty-two text messages and a number of phone calls since he had gone to sleep just a handful of hours earlier. Flipping through the messages with an increasing feeling of discomfort, Claus within moments realized how dire the situation was for him and his organization. The crisis had struck from out of nowhere.

In Denmark, and for foodies around the globe, Claus Meyer requires no introduction. He is the co-founder of Noma, the world's best restaurant in 2010, 2011, 2012 and 2014, according to *Restaurant* magazine. He was one of three TV hosts of *New Scandinavian Cooking*, which was aired in more than 130 countries and is estimated to have had a viewership of around 100 million people per episode.

That's just the tip of the iceberg. Since Claus Meyer returned from a year in France aged nineteen he has relentlessly been on a mission to transform the way we relate to food. A by-product of his calling has been a wide array of high-growth businesses, social projects, TV shows, movement-like initiatives and gourmet products. It's not an exaggeration to say that no one has done more for the revitalization of Nordic food culture than Claus Meyer. The reward has been a stellar reputation as one of Denmark's most trustworthy, admirable and impactful entrepreneurs. Most of his companies bear his name, and that's good for business. For decades the Meyer brand has been invincible, and the man himself seemed impeccable.

So Claus was equally surprised and devastated that morning in La Paz. A few months earlier he had come up with a new way to use food as a force for good. In collaboration with the Danish Prison and Probation Service, Claus had embarked on a project to establish a cooking school and restaurant in one of the most infamous Danish prisons, the state prison in Vridsløselille. The goal was rehabilitation. Claus had seen people from all walks of life build up their confidence, and find their calling, in front of the stove, so why not inmates?

Cooking doesn't require any formal education, sauce béarnaise won't discriminate, and what is more fulfilling than seeing a fellow human enjoy a meal you have made with your very own hands? Claus was convinced, and so was DR, the leading national television channel. When the reputable entrepreneur and gourmet evangelist entered the prison gates, so would DR. Rehabilitation documented for national television, presumably a win-win.

As a logical extension of the new alliance, Claus accepted an invitation from the Ministry of Social Affairs to participate in their outplacement programme. Some of the biggest Danish companies were already giving jobs to inmates. Claus agreed, and opened up the doors of one of his bakeries to a forty-three-year-old French convict on probation, Frank David Saksik. Claus had understood from his encounters with people from the prison service not to worry about what the inmates had done to deserve their imprisonment. That part had been up to the judge, and once the inmates had served their sentence, they had also settled their score with society. Claus refrained from asking Frank any questions about his past. The Ministry of Social Affairs eyed an opportunity to leverage Claus's status to brand their outplacement programme with a video of Claus and Frank side by side at a Meyers Bakery, talking about the 'match'.

For every crime there is a victim, and in Frank's case that was his ex girlfriend, Malene Duus. What Claus Meyer didn't know was that Frank and Malene hadn't exactly parted as friends. Frank struggled with the rejection, and shortly after the break-up he showed up at Malene's apartment in Copenhagen, presumably beat her unconscious with an iron pipe and dragged her body through her living room, took her in his arms and jumped out of the window of her third-floor apartment, eleven metres down onto the pavement.

They both sustained severe back injuries but miraculously survived. After three years Malene was still physically and emotionally suffering from the incident and unable to take a job. When she saw the man who had ruined her life on the internet, next to a celebrity chef, she felt humiliated and angry. She sat down and wrote a letter with her story and sent it to one of the biggest newspapers in Denmark, *Politiken* – which was happy to print the letter in full. With five hours of time difference, the reactions had built up to good old-fashioned hysteria back home in Denmark by the time Claus woke up in Bolivia.

The vast majority of commentators seemed to agree that Claus had made an awful mistake in giving Frank Saksik a job. Many went so far as to suggest a boycott of Meyer's companies, a proposal that was quickly gaining in popularity. There were some real nasty outbursts, too, including on Claus's fifteen-year-old daughter's Facebook page. Not exactly the reaction Claus had expected to his social work in reforming inmates. One Facebook comment had enough appeal to be quoted in a number of nationwide media outlets: 'I hope someone throws you out of the window, you shitty chef.'

'My head management were panicking and they all looked to me for how we should handle this,' Claus Meyer recalls. 'I instantly decided to write a personal reply to Malene and sent it to *Politiken*.' It was on the front page, online, two hours later. As time was of the essence, Claus only showed the letter to his wife, one colleague and a former police officer and friend, before he sent it off. Claus had made the right choice. His decision to write as a fellow human being, and a father of three girls, addressing Malene directly, in public, rather than as a corporate CEO, was rewarded. Some corners of the debate now became more nuanced. An increasing

number of people agreed with Claus that rehabilitation was a worthy cause – that if we do not
choose to keep inmates in prison forever or execute
them, then we have an interest in including them
in our society again, once they have served their
sentence.

Over the following days Claus woke up each
morning to fresh attacks from new angles in the
media. He fought them off as well as he could.
Cleverly he asked his friends to reply to some of the
attacks, rather than standing alone on the battle-
field. Criticism from a philosopher got matched by
Claus's friend and philosopher, Ole Thyssen. By ap-
plying himself, activating his network and putting
in the hours, Claus managed to get most Danes to
remember that they actually do believe that even
criminals deserve a second chance.

During those days both the board and the top
management in Claus's company urged Claus to
fire Frank Saksik. Since Frank was still on his probation period in the bakery, that would have been
an easy thing to do. And it most likely would have
put an effective end to the bombardment. To everyone's astonishment Claus's reply was a firm
no. Frank should stay. 'What signal would it be to
sacrifice something I existentially believed in, and
to let down an employee, to defend the profitability

of my company?' Claus asks rhetorically. 'Whatever I decided, it would be a decision I would have to live with for the rest of my life,' he states.

Thinking back on the hectic weeks, Claus remembers them as both incredibly stressful and full of clarity and beauty:

> It's one of the few times in my life that I really loved myself. My default is to be very critical with myself. I often think that I could be a better husband, a better father, a better friend, generally that I could do more or do better. But not those weeks. It was a very special feeling to have almost everyone against you – and still know that you were right.

Claus *was* right, and gradually public opinion came around. Most Danes believed that crimes like the one Malene Duus had been a victim of should be punished with much longer prison sentences. But they realized that didn't have anything to do with Claus Meyer and his rehabilitation project. Claus could again open his inbox and visit his Facebook page without being confronted with an angry mob. Little did he know that this had only been the beginning.

In Denmark, like in most parts of the world, the

tradition is that when you open up a restaurant you most likely won't have a contract with the unions. Unless you behave very badly, you will remain below their radar as long as you are a small fish. Claus now had more than 600 employees, and all the drama around the prison project had opened a crack. The man was on the radar, and no longer impeccable.

With perfect timing, the day before the premiere of the prison TV series, *Politiken* ran another full-page article about Claus Meyer, this time with a completely different focus: was the famous entrepreneur in reality a brutal employer, only caring about his profit, and using social projects as a smokescreen? They used more succinct copy, but the meaning was clear. Once again Claus was under severe attack, and this time much more dangerously. He was up against a lethal mix of a few unhappy employees and a more-than-willing media.

A union determined to use Claus's sudden vulnerability to increase its market share had launched a frontal attack. Claus hadn't known about the complaints coming from two of his bakeries, but of course that was no excuse. In a perfect world, he should have known, and he should have dealt with it. Within less than one painful week Claus knew

that he had to make a public apology, as well as ini-
tiate the process of getting an agreement with the
union.

Incidentally, I worked for Claus Meyer for almost two years, about a decade ago. The business
was smaller back then, and being in charge of business development I sat next to Claus in his private
villa, before the company had real headquarters. So
I know from first-hand experience that Claus is not
a brutal employer. In fact, I have never heard him
say anything unkind to anyone. I remember a
morning where he and I were driving to an important meeting together, and because I – his most recent hire – came to his house late, we both arrived
twenty-two minutes after the meeting was supposed to start. Of course, I could sense that Claus
wasn't happy about my sloppiness, but he remained
kind and when we finally arrived he apologized for
the delay without mentioning the reason. This was
the first and last time I was late.

After the first half-year in Claus's organization
it became clear to me that because Claus wasn't
the type of boss who could let anyone go, we had a
couple of managers that simply weren't up to the
job. I knew we needed to act on it, so I got the
board's support, and gradually I managed to

convince Claus for us to make the tough decision. If anyone knows how hard it is for Claus to be just a tiny bit brutal, even when it's justified and necessary, it's me.

At the same time it's fair to say that Claus's calling has always been about the quality of the food we eat, not about our work conditions. He doesn't wake up in the morning thinking about the length of work breaks, maybe because he himself really doesn't need many. It's not difficult for me to imagine how the dissatisfied employees in his bakeries have simply slipped his attention. Claus has always been more than happy to delegate management responsibilities, budget reviews, etc. – so that he himself could create new products, concepts and initiatives and engage in passionate conversations with colleagues and customers about those same issues. That's of course not an excuse; it's only an explanation. As a business owner, like most of us, Claus is not perfect. But profit-optimization and cynicism are absolutely not the underpinnings of his enterprise; rather the opposite, many insiders would claim.

Still, try to explain that when under attack by unions and sensational media outlets. Claus had stood up for the rehabilitation of ex prisoners, but he couldn't find a strong reason not to give in this time and sign a contract with the unions. 'What I learnt from this episode is that when the mission of your company is to change certain things for the better and especially when you are doing social projects in front of people's eyes, people expect you to be flawless within your own walls,' Claus recalls.

That's probably a really good point. I know of a lot of restaurant chains that haven't signed with the unions, but they are not doing charity or social work either. Because he engaged in rehabilitation, charity work in Bolivia, and a wide range of similar activities, in addition to having a pretty ambitious culinary agenda, Claus Meyer was expected by the public to live up to the highest possible standards in everything he did. When an area was revealed where his company's performance was only mediocre, on par with a not-that-impressive industry standard, then all hell broke loose. Claus learnt his lesson, accepted the realities and made amends.

Today the crisis is over, and Claus's company is stronger than ever. The newest adventure? A relocation of the whole family to New York to start up a food court inside Grand Central Station, a gourmet restaurant next door and a charity project in Brooklyn – alongside investments in two other new Manhattan restaurants created by Scandinavian chefs.

I shared Claus's story in great detail to illustrate as vividly as possible how crisis can hit unexpectedly. And, especially for leaders that are in the public arena, it can quickly become a merciless juggernaut, threatening to destroy everything we create as leaders.

With this dark cloud behind him, I asked Claus to share his top three pieces of advice for fellow leaders on how to deal with crises of this nature. Claus thinks for a few minutes, and then suggests:

First of all, apply yourself. Approach the situation as a human being, not as a corporate CEO. In a crisis there will be many emotions at play. Claus experienced the importance of daring to be authentic instead of hiding behind business jargon or letting someone else do the talking on his behalf. Everyone knew that Claus was the owner and the face of the company, and they wanted to hear from the man himself. When you get into a crisis, rise to the challenge, be real about it, and spend the time and effort that is needed to weather the storm.

Secondly, get help. Claus didn't wait for the experts to arrive before he made his first statements, but he surely did get them on board as soon as possible. Before a critical talk show on national television he had two PR advisers shout at him for a full hour with spotlights in his face – to prepare him for the heat he would take from the infamous interviewer he was about to meet on air.

Claus's third piece of advice is to think through the landscape you are navigating. Who are friends and who are opponents? What agendas are at play? In any kind of communication or PR crisis think through what your core message is – and then adapt it to the different stakeholders and media.

Whilst these reflections made a lot of sense to me, I felt that something was missing. I pictured myself in a similar situation, and the cold shiver down my spine revealed that even with the above advice, I didn't feel one bit up for the challenge, should something comparable ever happen to me. 'But . . .' I said and knew that I was keeping Claus longer than we had agreed, 'I still don't really get it. How could you keep your cool under such pressure? I mean, the newspapers were full of dirt about you. For a while it was as if everyone loved to hate you. How did you manage to sleep at night, how did you stay strong in the middle of this?' I wanted to know.

Claus turned silent and thoughtful, which happens sometimes but not often. This was apparently not a question he had been asked before. 'The truth is,' he finally said, 'there was some relief to being portrayed as an imperfect person. I never wanted people to view me as perfect, and that's definitely not how I think of myself. During those critical weeks the balance was restored, and though it was painful whilst it happened, I am actually glad it did.' Claus continues: 'In our company we talk about the fact that we are on a journey, that we want to become the best version of ourselves, that we can always become better. With this mindset mistakes and failures are not so dangerous. Leaders who portray themselves or their organizations as perfect have a lot more to lose than I had.'

Claus is vibrant, and the insights come to him as he speaks: 'Also, I don't walk around with the feeling that my life will be over if I lose my reputation and my business. I could enjoy myself without all of this, in a small house with my family, cultivating vegetables in the garden, and spending more time with friends. It's all about perspective.' I nod in silence and this second round of advice hits something deeper in me, and seems to be applicable to any kind of crisis a leader can face.

Still, the last point Claus shares with me is the one that gave me goosebumps when I biked back to my office through Copenhagen that Tuesday morning. Claus is intense when he looks me in the eyes and, full of clarity and dedication, says: 'Martin, I am a strong believer in forgiveness. After taking the heat, I expected people to forgive me. I couldn't imagine they wouldn't. Of course, there are a few idiots out there, but I am full of trust that generally people are good.'

So when you experience a crisis as a leader, remember that we are all imperfect, never lose your perspective, and trust that you will eventually be forgiven. Acknowledging our fallibility and learning from crisis will help us develop the mindset required to keep our leadership strong and authentic.

Practice

In the absence of a bigger crisis, find a small one to practice on. Something that is not going your way, an area in your life where something has blown up, or maybe someone is not happy with you.

Ask yourself: What is the right thing to do under these circumstances? Get input from a few wise friends so the solution you come up with is a solid and fair one. Then implement it, full of faith that it will all be okay in the end – that the world will notice your good intentions, and that a crisis is nothing other than an opportunity to improve. Like Claus, don't be afraid to admit mistakes. Also don't lie down flat when you are making a stand for something that is bigger than you.

10. Welcome, Uncertainty

Much of our life is spent on the cusp of uncertainty and ambiguity. And this is especially the case for leaders in today's world.

Whether you are an entrepreneur creating something from nothing, stepping into a new leadership role, or simply leading your organization in an ever-changing, increasingly complex and uncertain world, we can all agree on this fact: there is no precise blueprint. No roadmap. No promise of success. For some, this can be a paralysing reality. It's therefore important that we develop 'uncertainty muscles', not just to cope, but to thrive and to *create* on the edge of the unknown.

What follows is a story about one entrepreneur's journey, navigating not merely ripples, but tidal waves of uncertainty. Once that journey reached its end, a shift occurred – from being taunted, afraid and in pain, to letting go and being intrigued. As the story unfolds, we'll see how this leader managed to turn uncertainty, fear, doubt and ambiguity into fuel for brilliance and success. We hope these insights will inspire you to release the grip on any notion of a 'safe and certain path'. Rather, we hope you will welcome – indeed, lean into – uncertainty as a creative ground from which you can bring your leadership to life.

As he was getting off a plane in Austin, Texas, Jonathan noticed an odd fluttering and clicking sensation in his left ear. He had long been excited to go to the South-by-Southwest festival and tried hard not to take much notice of the strange sensation, thinking it would go away once his ears recovered from the cabin pressure. If you've ever been to this festival you will know that things can get loud, really loud at times. With upwards of 70,000 participants descending upon Austin, and a melange of activities around film, music, technology and entrepreneurship, you can only imagine the sensory overload!

Jonathan kept busy on the first day of the festival, all the while trying to shake off the sensation in his left ear. That first night in Austin he could barely sleep. The sound just wasn't going away and seemed to be getting worse, especially when he tried to lie down. He got through the rest of the festival, becoming increasingly tired and frustrated. He couldn't tell whether it was that the Geiger-like clicking and fluttering sensations were getting louder and louder or that he was simply becoming too exhausted and sleep-deprived to cope.

When he returned home to New York City, he consulted a series of doctors who ruled out some of the 'big, scary things' and told him to rest. 'Easier said than done!' he thought. Jonathan's doctors assured him that things should clear up soon. But one month after his trip to Austin, Jonathan woke up in the middle of the night with a loud, all-consuming high-pitched sound blasting in both of his ears.

'When I realized the sound was coming from the inside of my head, I just broke down,' he recalls.

Jonathan Fields was no stranger to uncertainty and anxiety. Early in his professional life, he had been an enforcement attorney at the Securities and Exchange Commission in New York City. He later joined a large law firm in Manhattan, doing things like raising hedge funds and working on mergers-and-acquisitions projects. Emergency surgery following a three-week stint working non-stop at the office was a sure signal that his body was rejecting his career, and that it was time for a change.

He left the corporate-finance world and returned to his earlier twin loves of entrepreneurship and wellness, building and growing a fitness business which he eventually sold. On 10 September 2001, Jonathan had taken a definitive step towards starting a new project he was very passionate about. He had signed a six-year lease for a floor in a building in Hell's Kitchen, midtown Manhattan. This was to become his new yoga centre. The next morning, on 9/11, Jonathan's city and the entire world was changed forever. 'New York was a horrifying place to be for quite some time after that,' Jonathan tells us. 'So here I was, I'd just signed a long lease for this space and my daughter was only three months old at the time. Despite the uncertainty, I decided to commit to the business and we created a space that was all about the community, a place where people could breathe, where we could find a sense of calm.' The business thrived. And after seven years Jonathan sold it and moved on to other projects.

Throughout his career, Jonathan had come to realize that 'in order to do something extraordinary, to create something from nothing, you have to not only be okay with uncertainty, but actually welcome it'. He became curious about how some people seemed to have an ability to *harness* uncertainty and use it as fuel for creativity. But for the vast majority, uncertainty plunges us into a dark cesspool of fear, doubt and anxiety. Which, to some of us, may sound more like cripplingly scary monsters than fuel for creativity and brilliance.

No risky business or entrepreneurial roller-coaster ride could have prepared Jonathan for this new challenge – figuring out just what to do with the piercing sound inside his head. The high-pitched scream in both of his ears was a clear sign that his doctors had been too optimistic. After a new battery of tests, Jonathan finally had a diagnosis: tinnitus. The good news was that he now knew what he was dealing with. The bad news: there's no cure or known cause of this condition, and it seemed unlikely that Jonathan would ever again find the quiet inside his mind.

Curious about the condition, I spent a few depressing hours scouring the internet for information on tinnitus. What I found was horrifying. Endless accounts of how impossible it was to live with tinnitus, and heartbreaking stories from family members losing their loved ones to suicide because they simply could no longer bear to live. One patient, after suffering with tinnitus for just three months, desperate to be either deaf or dead, stabbed himself in the heart.[1] Tinnitus, depression and suicide seemed to be tied up in a Gordian knot.

After more than one year of researching and

trying everything under the sun, from acupuncture, aromatherapy, vitamin supplements and 'miracle drugs' to all kinds of advice he found on online tinnitus forums, Jonathan saw his life heading in a terrible direction. A low point came when he had to tell his wife that he had developed a hypersensitivity to the frequency of her voice. The sound of her voice was scrambling his brain. 'Was it not enough that this cursed condition robbed me of my peace, would it also tear my family apart?' thought Jonathan, on the edge of despair. And here comes the scary thought: the dissonant clamour in his head, like an unwelcome house guest, was here to stay. For the rest of his days.

In his book *Mindfulness in Plain English*, Sri Lankan Buddhist monk Bhante Henepola Gunaratana explains our tendency to categorize our experiences and perceptions, and sheds light on the fixed habitual mental responses that follow this categorization.

We tend to categorize every perception or mental change into one of three 'mental pigeon holes', Gunaratana believes. Something is either good, bad or neutral. If the perception is labelled 'good', we tend to want to grab and hold on to it or repeat it as often as possible. If something is perceived as 'bad', we naturally work to deny and reject the experience.[2]

And that is what Jonathan did. Until, underneath the pain, fear and uncertainty, he was ready to discover a new perspective.

Rather than continuing to reject the sounds in his head, Jonathan started to ask a different question: 'If this is me, for life, if I have to live with this highly distressing thing and in a state of constant uncertainty of whether it will get better or worse, or if it will ever go away – how can I learn to be okay with it?'

He began to experiment with blending yoga practice, breathing exercises and what he knew of somatic psychology (a branch of psychology that deals with the mind–body connection), together with a daily mindfulness practice. 'Mindfulness,' Jonathan explains, 'can either be a sitting practice or an approach to everyday life.' He practised both. And, after many months of daily practice Jonathan noticed that whilst meditation didn't take the pain away, it did rewire the way his brain processed pain, such that it no longer stopped him from doing what he loved. Just how did he do it?

Initially the practice was to allow his awareness to focus on the sensations in his body, to notice

without judgment, then let them go. 'Classic meditation and mantra practices encourage you to focus
on one sensation – an anchor – and let everything
else go. Eventually you can evolve the practice into
what is called "open monitoring", where you invite
everything in, notice, then let it go, without need-
ing an anchor,' explains Jonathan.

'If, however, as you sit, the same sensation or
thought keeps coming at you, over and over again,
in classic meditation you are invited to explore
making that your anchor,' says Jonathan. In his
case, that one thing that kept coming at him was the
excruciating sound inside his head. It took months
of practice, gradually allowing the sound to become
the anchor for his meditation. Filled with pain and
anxiety, at times unable to breathe, Jonathan continued to practice until one day, as he was sitting,
he realized that his mind had gently and quite
organically drifted away from the sound. Finally,
the quiet inside his mind had returned, if only for a
few minutes.

It takes grit and gumption to go even deeper
into the very thing that torments you. With curiosity,
and a lot of trepidation, Jonathan decided to experiment with complete sensory deprivation. If all
stimuli were reduced to zero, would the sounds in
his head present louder?

The isolation tank was invented in the mid 1950s by John C. Lilly, a neuropsychiatrist at the US National Institute of Mental Health. The modern version is a dark, soundproof tank, inside which one can float in a mixture of Epsom salts and water at skin temperature. Of course the sound was there, loud as ever, but to Jonathan's surprise, in this complete isolation, with no other sensory input, he was fine with it. He had trained himself to be curious about it, and as he floated in the isolation tank, he no longer tried to resist the sound inside his head. Instead, he began to notice different frequencies blending together. Curiosity taking over, he thought, 'How fascinating! I wonder what they are here to teach me.'

Mindfulness was the tool which turned the painful torment inside his head into his greatest teacher. His journey into learning to live with tinnitus – not just to survive, but to have a good life – prepared Jonathan for work that is even closer to his heart. Today he does highly transformational work with leaders and entrepreneurs from all over the world. His current focus, the GoodLifeProject, is a global movement that inspires, educates, connects and supports mission-driven individuals in their quest to live better, more engaged, connected and aligned lives.

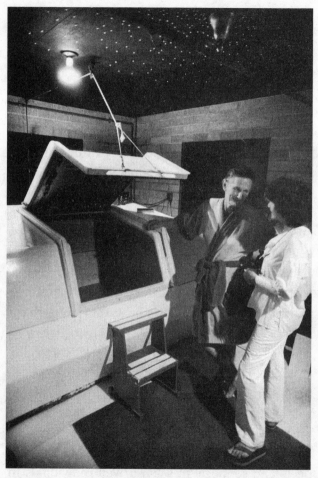

Dr John C. Lilly and his wife, Toni, stand next to an isolation chamber.

Whether you are a leader of one or a leader of many, you no doubt encounter uncertainty, fear and ambiguity on a daily basis. I know I do. The way we condition ourselves to cope with them is one of the greatest determinants of success in leadership and in life.

'The more you're able to tolerate ambiguity and lean into the unknown, the more likely you'll be to dance with it long enough to come up with better solutions, ideas and creations,' says Jonathan in our interview.

What does this mean in practical terms?

Jonathan showed us that the ability to handle uncertainty and the high level of fear that comes with it is not simply a matter of landing in the right gene pool. It's not something that either you're born with or you're not. And that's good news. This is a process, and there are in fact things we can all do to become, in Jonathan's words, 'uncertainty and fear alchemists'.

Practice
We invite you to experience uncertainty as an opportunity, rather than anxiously resist-ing it, or suffering through it. Bring mind-fulness and curiosity into the experience. Breathe through it. Relax into it. Stay with it

long enough to bring creative genius into your leadership.

We asked James Flaherty, founder of Integral Leadership LLC, to share with us one of the practical things he encourages his clients to do on a daily basis. To help you develop your capacity to sit in the middle of uncertainty without losing your centre, learn to work with the fear that arises when facing uncertainty. 'Take a deep, cleansing breath,' says James, 'and imagine that this fear is a guest. Invite it in as you would an old friend. Ask your guest: "What are you here to tell me?" Then pause, drop the storyline and the narrative surrounding this emotion, and focus on becoming aware of how fear actually feels in your body. Then watch its energy dissipate.'

Another practice we would recommend, to help build 'uncertainty muscles', is simple, harmless and can be quite fun. Go somewhere new. Leave your maps behind and switch off the GPS on your phone. Make sure you have plenty of time available so you can lose yourself in the maze of a new city. Needless to say this is a walking practice; you are not to do this whilst driving. Allow your intuition to take the lead. Take in everything. Notice sounds, textures, colours. Feel what it's like to navigate a new terrain, to approach uncertainty and the unknown with a sense of discovery and wonderment, rather than fear and anxiety.

11. Double Your Failure Rate

Failure, often seen as the opposite of success, is one of the most crippling shadow elements in leadership. The feeling of failing can make us doubt ourselves, it often compromises our dedication and energy, and in the worst cases it can stop us from moving forward. As such, failure deserves some attention. In this chapter we will examine the nature of failure and what it is really trying to tell us. The philosopher Nietzsche, bestselling author Elizabeth Gilbert and an American venture-capital firm are going to be our guides. But allow me to start with an episode from my own life.

In 2009, whilst attending a fancy conference for elite investors, I had an 'aha' moment. Truthfully I felt a bit phony being there. We had sold one of our businesses earlier that year, and on paper it could look like we belonged in this fine company. But the deal had been 90 per cent earn-out based, and one look at our bank account would reveal that we weren't really the target audience for this type of event. Curiosity had driven me there more than a genuine hunt for Series-A investment prospects. And I did surely learn something new, albeit something completely different than what I was expecting.

The parking lot was full of posh cars, the accommodation impeccable, the suits surrounding me undoubtedly very expensive. But all these privileged souls were feeling 'down' that beautiful summer day in June, complaining about their misfortune, and ranting on about how much money they had lost since the collapse of Lehman Brothers and the start of the financial crisis. It only took a couple of hours talking to them for me to realize that they felt like failures. This was a huge surprise to me because in my book they still looked pretty accomplished. How can it make a huge difference to a person's self-esteem whether he is good for 100 rather than 200 million dollars? These were prudent investors, and none of them were on the verge of bankruptcy. They had merely lost a chunk of the paper money they had easily made on a heated stock market in preceding years. In my view that shouldn't be such a big deal.

What I learnt that day is how relative the notions of success and failure really are. And I have since witnessed many more examples of the same phenomenon. If a leader used to be the CEO of a 10,000-person company, has had to change jobs and is now 'only' in front of 1,000 employees then there is a big risk that she will have feelings of failure. Even though very few people ever get entrusted with such a big responsibility. Many of us have a habit of judging ourselves in comparison to what we have previously accomplished – or maybe even to what we once *dreamed* of achieving. With this mindset, the risk that we will have feelings of failure and disappointment as we get older increases.

Elizabeth Gilbert knows this dynamic better than anyone. In February 2006, when she was thirty-six, Penguin published her book *Eat, Pray, Love*. The memoir went straight to the *New York Times* bestseller list, where it stayed for an astonishing 187 weeks. Columbia Pictures purchased the movie rights, and in 2010 Elizabeth could witness Julia Roberts starring as her, accompanied by Javier Bardem playing the Brazilian businessman whom Elizabeth had fallen in love with during her stay in Bali. On Amazon the book has 3,718 reviews, which commands respect from anyone with experience in book marketing.

Now, how did Elizabeth Gilbert feel about all this success? In February 2009, whilst working on the sequel to *Eat, Pray, Love,* she gave a TED talk in Long Beach, California. The talk has had more than 10 million views, and is on the list of the twenty most popular TED talks of all time.

During her eighteen minutes on stage, Elizabeth shares with her audience that she is well aware she can probably never match, let alone top, the success she has experienced, at a rather young age, with *Eat, Pray, Love*. The most common question that people ask her is if she is afraid that from now on everything she does is going to look like a failure compared to that one massive win. She reveals that yes, she is afraid of that.

Then she moves on to tell how she has found a way to deal with the fear. The trick is, she says, to view your *genius* as something external to you, instead of as a quality within you. Like something divine that may be bestowed upon you. All you can do is show up and be grateful when this divine genius alights upon you. As humans our part of the job is to show up every day, and do our best. The rest is not up to us. This mindset will keep you sane, Elizabeth promises, and she goes on to share a handful of really inspiring examples.

Elizabeth did put out the sequel, *Committed*, in 2011. To this date it has 575 reviews on Amazon, which by most standards is very impressive, but of course a far cry from the mania that surrounded *Eat, Pray, Love*.

There is another reason that failure, and success, are such relative perceptions: we have a tendency to compare ourselves to people in our immediate surroundings. It's been said that a rich man is a man who owns more than his neighbour. I think we all recognize this pattern from our own lives; I know that I do.

When I was in my early twenties, I tried to get my own business off the ground, but failed again and again, for years. Going back to school, then joining a top management consulting firm only augmented my tendency to compare myself with those around me – classmates, fellow consultants, the entrepreneurs I read about in the media.

Since then I have learnt that feelings of failure are always going to be part of the journey – especially for those who are stepping up as leaders, taking risks and creating something from nothing. Some initiatives will go well, others will flunk. As long as we show up, putting our best effort into doing what we've been put on this planet to do, *then that's success in itself.*

In addition to being *relative*, existing predominantly in the eye of the beholder, success and failure are *inseparable*. Without taking risks, we are not going to accomplish much. But taking a risk by definition involves a high probability of failure. Ninety per cent of all start-ups are said to fail, but still millions of people quit their job every year to start their own thing. Progress, innovation and ultimately our societies are dependent on such risk-taking, and when it goes well, it makes for great press. But there cannot be any success stories without many more cases of hardship that only lead to failure. This is true on a nationwide level, on a company level, and for all of us as individuals.

When you see an opportunity, do you go for it, even though you might fail? Or do you play it safe? In the famous words of the Danish philosopher Søren Kierkegaard: 'To dare is to lose one's footing momentarily. Not to dare is to lose oneself.'

The most successful leaders know this – and have found ways to deal with failure, welcome it and learn from it, rather than to try to escape it.

Humour, for example, can be a great way to deal with failure.

Bessemer Venture Partners (BVP) is the oldest venture capital firm in the United States, founded in 1911 by Henry Phipps with his share of the proceeds from the sale of Carnegie Steel. Today, BVP has seven offices around the world, has been part of 116 Initial Public Offerings and has $4 billion under management, investing in early-stage and hyper-growth start-ups. Their portfolio boasts household names such as LinkedIn, Skype, Staples, Yelp, Pinterest and Shopify. Sounds like a stellar success story? It is indeed, but BVP is – like any venture-capital company – also a tale of dozens of bad judgments and missed opportunities. The amazing thing about BVP is that they share their failures openly. On their website there is a tab called 'Anti-portfolio', at first glance a rather strange term. When you click on it, you will find a long list of iconic companies that BVP has turned down for investment. It's a hilarious read!

FACEBOOK
Jeremy Levine spent a weekend at a corporate retreat in the summer of 2004 dodging persistent Harvard undergrad Eduardo Saverin's rabid pitch. Finally, cornered in a lunch line, Jeremy delivered some sage advice: 'Kid, haven't you heard of Friendster? Move on. It's over!'

GOOGLE
Cowan's college friend rented her garage to Sergey and Larry for their first year. In 1999

and 2000 she tried to introduce Cowan to 'these two really smart Stanford students writing a search engine'. Students? A new search engine? In the most important moment ever for Bessemer's anti-portfolio, Cowan asked her, 'How can I get out of this house without going anywhere near your garage?'

APPLE

BVP had the opportunity to invest in pre-IPO secondary stock in Apple at a $60M valuation. BVP's Neill Brownstein called it 'outrageously expensive'.

EBAY

'Stamps? Coins? Comic books? You've GOT to be kidding,' thought Cowan. 'No-brainer pass.'

TESLA

In 2006 Byron Deeter met the team and test-drove a roadster. He put a deposit on the car, but passed on the negative-margin company, telling his partners, 'It's a win-win. I get a great car and some other VC pays for it!' The company passed $30B in market cap in 2014. Byron is still on the waiting list for a Model X.

BVP explains its decision to keep track of, and openly list, its failures in this way:

> We would like to honour these companies – our 'anti-portfolio' – whose phenomenal success inspires us in our ongoing endeavours to build growing businesses. Or, to put it another way: if we had invested in any of these companies, we might not still be working.

Humour has a way of dispelling blame and allows us to learn from the past, without letting failure knock us down. It's not always appropriate, but when we can take a step back and make light of the situation, our relationship with failure is reframed.

If self-deprecating humour is not your style, there's another way that might be helpful: view your failures through a philosophical lens.

In his book *The Consolations of Philosophy*, Swiss-British writer, thinker and founder of The School of Life, Alain de Botton, examines why Nietzsche was such a big advocate for hardship and humiliation. In his legendary book *The Will to Power*, Nietzsche declares:

To those human beings who are of any concern to me I wish suffering, desolation, sickness, ill-treatment, indignities – I wish that they should not remain unfamiliar with profound self-contempt, the torture of self-mistrust, the wretchedness of the vanquished.[1]

With a flair for drama, what Nietzsche intends to explain to us is that *failure and pain are necessary for growth* and therefore for any kind of real fulfilment. In one of his other books, *The Gay Science*, where he famously declares the death of God, Nietzsche continues to explain his thinking:

Examine the lives of the best and most fruitful people and peoples and ask yourselves whether a tree that is supposed to grow to a proud height can dispense with bad weather and storms; whether misfortune and external resistance, some kinds of hatred, jealousy, stubbornness, mistrust, hardness, avarice and violence do not belong among the favourable conditions without which any great growth even of virtue is scarcely possible.[2]

Poetic and dramatic, yes, but according to Alain de Botton, still very relevant as a contemporary consolation strategy in times of difficulty. In the words of de Botton:

> Why? Because no one is able to produce a great work of art without experience, nor achieve a worldly position immediately, nor be a great lover at the first attempt; and in the interval between initial failure and subsequent success, in the gap between who we wish one day to be and who we are at present, must come pain, anxiety, envy and humiliation. We suffer because we cannot spontaneously master the ingredients of fulfilment.[3]

You might object that you have actually already accomplished a lot, without suffering and anxiety. Such a perspective can indicate one of two explanations. Either you are already very good at dealing with failure, keeping strong and positive when you meet it, or else you haven't yet met hardship and setbacks of any significance, and you have up until now been dealt a lucky hand.

A friend of mine belonged in the second category. He was from a loving family, had always been very popular, including with the ladies, and without much effort he had received a stellar education.

He went on to land his dream job and hook up with the woman of his dreams. They created the perfect home. It was easy to think this guy had never seen a rainy day. Then within half a year his dad unexpectedly passed away, his girlfriend got a rare and scary disease and he lost his job. What my friend learnt during that year was that hardship sooner or later catches up with all of us. None of us get a free ride. Luckily he was strong enough to cope and grew remarkably on the back of the pain and the setbacks.

When you think about it, all these characteristics of failure are very encouraging. Because failure comes for all of us; because it is relative rather than absolute, and completely inseparable from success; because it is the greatest teacher around, we don't need to torment ourselves, and run away in fear, when we stare it in the eye. We should do our best to succeed in our endeavours, but when we meet failure along the way, it's a friend we are meeting, not an enemy.

Practice
The next time you experience feelings of failure, take a step back, carve out an hour for some introspection and ask yourself the following questions:

- Was there some part of the incident/ project that actually worked well?
- Imagine you could start it all over again. How would you go about it knowing what you know today?
- Visualize what happens when you try again with your new approach, and picture yourself being successful this time, and how good that feels.

Now that you have learnt from the failure, and connected with an altered approach and a successful outcome, ask yourself *What will be the optimal next step from here?* Then make a plan that involves a specific action you can take today.

12. On Ego and the Forces of Glamour

Picture this scene. The start-up team we had been working with had been making excellent progress in our accelerator programme. In a very short period of time they generated huge growth, getting lots of positive media attention and making good progress in securing follow-on investment. Then it all came to a screeching halt.

A series of incidents led to the need for us to have a serious conversation. The topic was whether we should reach out to all of the investors we introduced to this start-up and let them in on a vital piece of information: the start-up CEO's ego was getting out of hand. We saw it coming, but didn't understand the severity of the situation until the day both of his co-founders quit. How could we not alert the investors to hold off on signing those term sheets?

We have all been in some variation of this situation. Dealing with mischief created by the ego — ours or other people's. The ego is a cross we must all bear. So the question is how to recognize when the ego is running the show and how to deal with it.

A number of researchers and theorists have explored the dynamic between ego and leadership. David Marcum and Steven Smith called a leader's ego 'the invisible line item on a company's profit-and-loss statement', suggesting that it can be a most expensive liability. But if properly understood, our ego can also be a great asset.[1] In their book, *Egonomics: What Makes Ego Our Greatest Asset (or Most Expensive Liability)*, Marcum and Smith make a compelling case that it is the ego which sparks the drive to achieve, to create something new, to say 'I can do this better' or 'I can solve this problem'. The ego can also provide the energy and tenacity needed to face adversity. They do caution that it must be balanced with a healthy dose of humility.

These are all great examples of how the ego can assist in leadership. However, as this part of the book is dedicated to exploring the shadow elements, let's look more closely at the ways in which the ego is a liability.

C. G. Jung, Freud's former protégé, noted that 'It is a remarkable fact that a life lived entirely from the ego is dull, not only for the person himself but for all concerned.'[2]

Not just dull, but also dangerous, we would say. Especially in today's world of hyper-transparency and high expectations of our leaders.

So what then is the ego?

According to Freud, our psyche is made up of three parts: the first part, the ego ('I' in Latin), mediates between the other two parts: the id (instincts) and the super-ego (ethics). To Freud, the ego is the 'organized part of the personality' and works to please the id's drives and desires, whilst navigating within the boundaries set by the super-ego.

C. G. Jung, on the other hand, described the ego as a 'complex of ideas which constitute the centre of one's field of consciousness'. The ego, suggests Jung, emerged gradually out of unconsciousness and as such is 'a differentiated aspect of the collective unconscious', a sort of projection devised by the unconscious, and should not be confused with the Self, which is the subject of one's 'total psyche'.

Developmental psychology suggests that the awakening of the ego and therefore the emergence of the conscious self happens between eighteen months and four years of age, when the child becomes aware of him-/herself as a separate entity from the mother. So it is very likely that we don't remember what it's like not to have an ego.

For clarification, let's try this as a metaphor. The

ego is like man's best friend. You spend a lot of time together. And your best friend would do just about anything for you. Not intending to do disservice to our beloved quadruped friends, the ego is like a dog. It's always by your side, protecting you, unabashed in its display of affection and loyalty, making you feel better after a long day at work, begging to be petted, and making friends with other puppies (egos) at the dog park. You get the picture.

But, sometimes, your best friend turns into a scavenger dog, which, as Marianne Williamson, *New York Times* bestselling author, poetically said, 'seeks out every scrap of evidence of our brother's guilt'.[3] This means that the ego is all too happy to find fault, judge and criticize others.

The ego is tethered to you, like a loyal puppy on a leash, but it is not *you*. It's not who you really are.

The ego undoubtedly served an important function in the evolution of our species, otherwise we wouldn't have it. The reason *why* we have an ego is a question you may enjoy exploring. We won't go into that exploration here. Rather, let us consider how the ego can cause mischief for leaders, and how we can begin to take our leadership beyond the ego.

Because the ego is a separate self – a differentiated aspect of the collective – it keeps us separate from others, encouraging us to compete, defend and, when deemed necessary, to attack and seek revenge. In more subtle ways, the ego seeks validation and attention. Lots of it! The ego is often afraid and has to work really hard to 'feel' good. The attachment to self-importance, pride and the need for validation propels the ego into something which author and spiritual leader Ocean WhiteHawk calls 'the forces of glamour'.

Wait. What is glamour? And what's it doing in a leadership book?

'Glamour,' Ocean says, 'is a force field, a fog or haze, which stops you from seeing reality as it is. Because glamour distorts perception, when you are *in glamour* your interpretation is inaccurate. And if the interpretation is inaccurate, your response will also be faulty. So glamour prevents us from seeing something clearly. Glamour blocks our light, or understanding. It is in fact a world problem.'

'But, I'm not one to be glamorous or flashy,' you might object. And you would be right to associate the notion of glamour with opulence and today's attention-seeking, celebrity-elevating culture. However, we are using glamour in a different sense: as a fog into which our ego wanders much too often, and in ways that may not always be so obvious.

In truth, glamour comes from a place of lack.

Though at times it may seem harmless, the ego's entanglement is mighty.

'Glamour is bred in the emotional body, the desire body – desiring to be famous, to have a high profile, to be successful, to be the centre of attention, to be well known . . . Desiring to be anything other than who and what you already are,' explains Ocean.

Here are some quick examples profiling fictional characters, to help illustrate what we mean by being in the fog of glamour.

John is the CEO of a company he founded decades ago. He knows his industry better than anyone else. Over the years he's seen it all and worked with lots of different people. Because his company operates in an industry with low employee retention rates, rather than figuring out how to retain his employees, he has developed an unfortunate habit of complaining about them. In fact, he cannot wait for someone in his organization to make a mistake so that he can have a reason to complain about the misdeed and the perceived loss that it has caused. His ego is nurtured by finding fault in others. This is an example of being *in glamour*. Knowing that a leader sets the tone for what are acceptable behaviours in an organization, it's easy to guess the resulting culture in John's company.

Jane is a young consultant. She's well-educated, smart, friendly, charismatic and has a wide network of friends and contacts. She likes to bring people together and often creates opportunities to showcase her charismatic personality, in other words, her ego. Outside of social gatherings, Jane's behaviour tells a different story. She has a difficult time following through on commitments and often finds herself jumping from one project to another, reaching for the next big thing.

Joe is a serial entrepreneur. He claims he's bootstrapping his business with limited funds, and often has a hard time paying the bills. But he insists on fine dining and luxury hotels when attending conferences or meeting investors.

Ana is a middle-aged mother of two. She spends much of her time sharing on social media all sorts of stories about the not-so-fortunate happenings both in her kids' lives and in the world at large. Her followers comment and lament every heartbreaking incident, and are likely inclined to adopt the depressing attitude that life's a crapshoot, the world is a battleground, and it's all going down the drain.

I come home from work and spend thirty minutes subjecting my beloved to a diatribe about how awful my journey was, crowded Tube, rude people, sweaty armpits and all. Rather than being present and connecting with my beloved, I not only relive the experience, but drag him into that energy as well.

Dramatics, of the woe-is-me, look-what-happened-to-me-or-my-kids variety are a sign that the person concerned is stuck in the fog of glamour. There's glamour in busyness and self-importance. There's also glamour in spiritual aspiration. Dr Martin Laird, priest and author, cautions that spirituality can become 'champagne for the ego', reminding us that the ego's need to be centre-stage is mighty, and there are many traps.[4] Imagine a young life-coach feeling proud to have discovered the power to remove a psychological block for someone, or facilitating some change, then boasting about it. That is glamour. Or the spiritual teacher who is overly concerned with his status and intellectual property. That too is glamour.

Glamour throws us into a sticky pool of feelings, commentaries, judgments, opinions, gossip – all tricky things that keep us entangled and at the mercy of our ego's tantrums. If I live in the fog of glamour, I perpetuate more of it in the world. Being in glamour affects my ability to be present, and this of course has a tremendous impact on how I interact with those around me. Not exactly the best platform for leadership.

Remember where glamour comes from: a place of lack that occurs when the ego says: 'As I am, I'm not enough.' Being in glamour ensures that when we interact with others, we meet in fear, ego-to-ego, mask-to-mask. Of course the experience may satisfy the ego temporarily. 'But at the end of the day, when you're alone with no one to praise, acknowledge, feel sorry for you, or otherwise pay attention to you, you are left with just yourself. And that's the voice that counts,' says Ocean.

If we want to avoid becoming what *New York Times* bestselling author Tim Ferriss calls 'a Dow Joneser, someone whose self-worth is dependent on things largely outside of their control', ego and glamour must be addressed.[5]

What to do about it?

There are some traditions that place great emphasis on 'burning' the ego. In his book *Hvad er Ego? (What is Ego?)*, Bo Heimann shares a story about holy men in India that have spent their entire lives working on eradicating their ego. They ended up practically in a vegetative state, unable to care for themselves.

Because the ego has a bad reputation in their culture, people respect and look after these 'egoless' men. Don't expect this to happen in the West. So don't try to burn or shatter the ego. It will fight for its survival and cling to you with much tenacity.

Rather than declaring war on our ego, we must – as Jung suggests – 'by hook or by crook achieve a higher level of consciousness'. We must evolve our understanding, our awareness, in order to overcome our preoccupation with self-centred needs and self-serving ideas, and shift our focus towards being more concerned with benefiting others and benefiting all of life. 'Because,' says Ocean, 'our true nature is complete, it does not seek opportunities for glamour.'

We ask you, what would it be like *to lead* from this place?

But alas, in the age of the selfie, how can one be selfless?

In fact, being focussed on serving and benefiting others soothes the soul and brings us in alignment with our true nature.

As leaders we must learn to see through this profound identification with the ego. It is only in the light of awareness that our inner teacher feels safe enough to speak its truth. With awareness we can cultivate detachment from the ego's grip, and evolve our consciousness.

Eastern wisdom teaches us that attachment – to

our viewpoint, our ideas, likes and dislikes – is the source of all our suffering. Being 'attached' means being in the story, in the narrative and our judgment about a situation.

One of the most effective mindfulness techniques for developing awareness and cultivating detachment is to become a gentle witness, a silent observer of the ego's likes and dislikes, and to notice where attachment happens. This is an ongoing journey, not a one-time task. As such, it requires perseverance, determination and humility.

You may be starting to worry that being detached will render you unable to achieve your dreams. To be clear, being detached does not mean that I close my heart and don't care. Far from it. Whenever I struggle with attachment – to a goal, project or desired outcome – I find it easier to let go and practise detachment if I reflect on some of Parker J. Palmer's wisdom. An author and activist for social change, Palmer invites us to consider that our deepest calling is to grow into our own authentic selfhood. As we do so, we will find the joy we all seek as well as our path of authentic service.

Only when we move beyond the fragility and absurdity of the ego can we evolve our consciousness. But evolve we shall. As Palmer says, we must 'shed our skin in the service of transformation', if we are to bring about change – which we believe is the great task of leadership.

Practice

We could, and most likely will, spend our entire lives observing the ego and balancing its antics with healthy doses of humility. Here is perhaps the most elegant shortcut, or hack, we've come across in handling the ego and avoiding being pulled into the fog of glamour. This comes from author and spiritual leader Ocean WhiteHawk.

Close your eyes and take a deep cleansing breath in. Then visualize a horse-drawn carriage. Make it as lovely as you feel inclined to . . . Now, with your mind's eye, see this carriage as your physical body. The horses pulling your carriage represent your mind, and they are powerful, pulling in all directions.

Then, as you look more closely at the driver of your carriage, you notice that he is wearing a blindfold, earplugs and a tape over his mouth. And you wonder, 'How on earth does he know where to lead my carriage?' This driver is the ego, or personality. It is blind, deaf and mute, and yet it is the driver – or CEO – of your life.

Do yourself a loving favour and write a letter of termination to this driver. Thank him for his services and firmly dismiss him. Once you've done that, go ahead and appoint the alternative driver. He is wise, generous, compassionate, and his vision is unencumbered. Congratulations. You've just welcomed your soul into the driver's seat.

Repeat this visualization every time you observe your ego taking over.

Afterword

It can be fascinating to observe how leadership happens in every human interaction. At a parent meeting at the school, during an unexpected event in the neighborhood, at the dinner table at home, during a client meeting at work. Being creatures of habit, we often fall into our respective roles without even noticing it. We become the parent with all the critical questions for the school principal, the passive bystander to a violent episode in the subway, or maybe the thoughtful employee with all the right answers but no desire to speak up at meetings.

The process of writing this book has helped us see how in many of life's circumstances we ourselves are just as often followers as we are leaders. Maybe you are too. And this is only natural. No one should be leading all the time. In a world full of aware, informed and empowered people, a more valuable dynamic is that of both giving and receiving leadership. Offer your leadership when you feel that it can be of service. In this way, it will come from a deeper place.

This has been our focus: impactful, constructive and wholesome leadership. The twelve lessons we shared seem to us to be the most profound ones, and many of them are often overlooked. Our mission has been to inspire you to unleash your leadership powers in a way that will serve you long term, as well as being a positive contribution to all of us.

Go ahead. Lead with a giant heart and gentle spirit.

Homework

1. Is There Something You Really, Really Care About?

For centuries we've been asking existential questions to help us understand our purpose and make sense of our life experiences, particularly the ones that have challenged us. There are countless tools and frameworks which are meant to help us discover and communicate purpose; one such framework that is growing in popularity, especially in America, is Simon Sinek's Golden Circle, which he introduces in his book *Start With Why*. To get the essence of Simon's framework, we suggest viewing his TED talk: 'How Great Leaders Inspire Action'.

For a more contemplative journey, Parker J. Palmer, author and founder of the Center for Courage & Renewal, explores these questions with wisdom and compassion in his 1999 book *Let*

Your Life Speak: Listening for the Voice of Vocation.
What we love about this book is his invitation to
pause, be still and listen deeply to the voice of your
soul: 'Before you tell your life what you intend to
do with it, listen for what it intends to do with you.'
Also essential reading is Viktor E. Frankl's short
but monumental book *Man's Search for Meaning.*

2. Mind the Body

'A human being is just that, energy, waves, pat-
ters, rhythms. Nothing more. Nothing less,' says
internationally renowned theatre director, dancer
and author Gabrielle Roth in her refreshing book,
Sweat Your Prayers: Movement as Spiritual Practice.
This, together with Susannah and Ya'Acov Darling
Khan's *Movement Medicine: How to Awaken, Dance
and Live Your Dreams*, have given us the courage to
suggest dance and movement as important tools
to add to your leadership kit. Have a look at these
writings, or better yet, put your body in motion
and experience a 5Rhythms class available widely
across the world.

For a closer look at the practical applications of
Somatics – the unity of language, action, emotions and meaning – to leadership, we recommend

Richard Strozzi-Heckler's book: *Being Human at Work: The Art of Bringing Somatic Intelligence into Your Professional Life.*

We found Anodea Judith's *Eastern Body, Western Mind: Psychology and the Chakra System as a Path to Self* a comprehensive system for understanding imbalances within the energy centres (chakras) in the body – what causes them and what can be done to restore balance. If you are up for an exploration of the chakras through Jungian psychology, this is a good place to start.

3. Unleash Your Curiosity

To boost your curiosity and stretch your mind, check out WaitButWhy.com. The blogger, Tim Urban, takes his readers on a head-spinning journey across topics such as: are we alone in the universe, what should we make of artificial intelligence, and also more down-to-earth questions like why some people are always late.

The BBC and Science Channel series *Wonders of the Solar System* (2010), *Wonders of the Universe* (2011) and *Wonders of Life* (2013), all hosted by physicist Brian Cox, are incredible documentaries sure to unleash curiosity and inspire.

4. Infuse Your Leadership With 'Ecosophy'

He is considered one of the most important and rel-evant voices in modern environmentalism and the founder of 'deep ecology'. In his 2008 book *Ecology, Community and Lifestyle: Outline of an Ecosophy*, Arne Naess outlines strategies and ideas sure to inspire any thoughtful environmentalist.

In *Gaia & God: An Ecofeminist Theology of Earth Healing*, Rosemary Radford Ruether explores the centuries-old beliefs that have influenced our rela-tionship with the earth and how these beliefs have led to our current ecological crisis. Echoing the wisdom of the elders in Tejakula village, north-ern Bali, Redford Ruether invites her readers to transform the 'interrelations of men and women, humans and earth, humans and the divine, the divine and the earth'.

5. Master the Art of Communication

Ashridge Business School leadership expert Megan Reitz's *Dialogue in Organisations: Developing Rela-tional Leadership* (2015) explores how leaders need to start having meaningful conversations, and to meet in dialogue rather than monologue.

Steven Covey's 1987 book *Seven Habits of Highly Effective People* is a must-read, if you haven't read it already. The principle of 'seek first to understand then to be understood' will make a tremendous difference in your leadership and your life.

6. Define Your Riverbanks

In his 2006 book *Setting the Table: The Transforming Power of Hospitality*, legendary New York City restaurateur Danny Meyer shares his wisdom on what it took to create the award-winning corporate culture across his restaurants and business units. Clarity of the company's non-negotiable core values along with what Danny calls 'constant, gentle pressure' are some of his preferred leadership techniques.

We would also encourage you to look at *The Culture Cycle: How to Shape the Unseen Force That Transforms Performance*, by James Heskett.

7. Decision-making is a Team Sport

We mention Zappos as the most prominent experiment with implementing Holacracy. Google

'Zappos holacracy', if you want to keep up with the latest on their transition. For a deeper dive into this narrative, take a look at Brian J. Robertson's 2015 book *Holacracy: The New Management System for a Rapidly Changing World*.

If you happen to be in Copenhagen, wander over to Freetown Christiania to experience this controversial cultural phenomenon and perhaps reflect on how you might do better. If a trip to Denmark isn't on your radar, a close second is the 2014 documentary film *Christiania: 40 Years of Occupation*, directed by Richard Jackman and Robert Lawson.

8. Grow Your Appetite for Altruism

If you are inspired to go deeply into the study of altruism, in nearly 700 pages Matthieu Ricard's *Altruism: The Power of Compassion to Change Yourself and the World* offers a most comprehensive argument for the power of altruism.

In his TEDx Cambridge talk 'How to Buy Happiness', Michael Norton shares research on how being altruistic with our money can in fact make us happy.

9. Leadership During Crisis

We suggest a look at Matias Dalsgaard's 2014 *Don't Despair: Letters to a Modern Man (Your Best Self)*. The short, existential letter format makes it a powerful yet accessible read.

10. Welcome, Uncertainty

If you were inspired by his story, take a look at Jonathan Fields's *Uncertainty: Turning Fear and Doubt into Fuel for Brilliance*. It may just transform your relationship with uncertainty.

11. Double Your Failure Rate

For a positive and reassuring approach to failure, we suggest taking a look at John C. Maxwell's *Failing Forward: Turning Mistakes into Stepping Stones for Success*.

We were heartened by Alain de Botton's 'Consolation for Difficulties' chapter in his bestselling book *The Consolations of Philosophy*.

Finally, Elizabeth Gilbert's 2014 TED talk 'Success, Failure and the Drive to Keep Creating' is a must.

12. On Ego and the Forces of Glamour

In their 2008 book *Egonomics: What Makes Ego Our Greatest Asset (or Most Expensive Liability)*, David Marcum and Steven Smith present arguments for both the upside and the downside of a leader's ego.

The chapter titled 'The Wisdom that Realizes Egolessness' in Sogyal Rinpoche's spiritual classic *The Tibetan Book of Living and Dying* provides an enlightening description of the ego as a 'false and ignorantly assumed identity' that hangs on to a makeshift image of ourselves. Spend some time with his enormously important book, not just to further your understanding of the ego, but as a helpful manual for life and death.

Notes

Introduction

1 A definition of the 'bystander effect' can be found on *Psychology Today*: www.psychologyto day.com/basics/bystander-effect

1. Is There Something You Really, Really Care About?

1 'Why Thousands Are Saying "It's About More Than the Coffee"', by John Sweeney. Published in the *Huffington Post*, November 2014.

2. Mind the Body

1 'Do Schools Kill Creativity?' TED talk by Sir Ken Robinson.

2 'Sleep Drives Metabolite Clearance from the Adult Brain', *Science*, 18 October 2013, Vol. 342, no. 6156, pp. 373–7. www.sciencemag.org/content/342/6156/373

3 'Recommended Amount of Sleep for a Healthy Adult: A Joint Consensus Statement of the American Academy of Sleep Medicine and the Sleep Research Society', *Sleep*, vol. 38, 6, 2015.

4 Alain de Botton, *The Consolations of Philosophy* (London: Hamish Hamilton, 2000), p. 231.

5 Quote often attributed to Stanley Keleman, creator of Formative Psychology.

6 Joe Dispenza, TEDx talk at Tacoma, Washington: www.youtube.com/watch?v_symbol>=W81CHn4l4AM

7 J. Andrew Armour, M.D., PhD, *Neurocardiology: Anatomical and Functional Principles*, ebook.

8 Ibid.

9 Michael D. Gershon, M.D., *The Second Brain: A Groundbreaking New Understanding of Nervous Disorders of the Stomach and Intestine* (New York: Harper, 1998).

10 Dr Bruce Lipton, *Biology of Belief* (London: Hay House Publishing, 2008), p. 61.

11 'There are 37.2 Trillion Cells in Your Body', by Rose Eveleth, *Smithsonian*, 24 October 2013. www.smithsonianmag.com/smart-news/there

-are-372-trillion-cells-in-your-body-4941473
/?no-ist

12 David R. Hawkins, M.D., PhD, *Power vs Force:
The Hidden Determinants of Human Behaviour*
(London: Hay House Publishing, 2004), p. 214.

4. Infuse Your Leadership with 'Ecosophy'

1 Randolph S. Churchill, *Winston S. Churchill,
Youth, 1874–1900* (London: Heinemann, 1966),
pp. 94–5.

2 Peter M. Senge, Joseph Jaworski, C. Otto
Scharmer, Betty Sue Flowers, *Presence: Exploring profound change in people, organizations and
society*, (London: Nicholas Brealey Publishing,
2005), p. 64.

3 Ibid., p. 65.

4 For those interested in experiencing a Deep
Time Walk, Professor Nichols recommends con-
tacting the Schumacher College (www.schum
achercollege.org.uk), or Global Generation, a
London-based organization dedicated to increasing awareness of our connection with the
natural world (www.globalgeneration.org.uk).

5. Master the Art of Communication

1 Trudi West, faculty member at Ashridge Business School, *The Challenge of Leading: Insights from the Clipper Round the World Race,* June 2013. www.ashridge.org.uk/getattachment/Faculty -Research/Research/Current-Research/Research -Projects/Clipper-Research/Clipper-Report_Ex ecutive-Summary.pdf
2 Barry Johnson, PhD, *Polarity Management: Identifying and Managing Unsolvable Problems* (Amherst: HRD Press, 1992).
3 *Chief Executive Legal Guide,* www.gibsondunn .com/publications/Documents/CEOLegalGuide -WhiteCollarChapter.pdf

6. Define Your Riverbanks

1 US Bureau of Labor and Statistics, 2013.
2 'Will Investors Put the Lid on The Container Store's Generous Wages?' Susan Befriend for *Bloomberg Businessweek,* 19 February 2015. www .bloomberg.com/news/articles/2015-02-19/con tainer-store-conscious-capitalism-and-the-perils -of-going-public

3   John Mackey and Raj Sisodia, *Conscious Capitalism: Liberating the Heroic Spirit of Business* (Boston: Harvard Business Review Press, 2013), p. 232.

8. Grow Your Appetite for Altruism

1   'Koppel Report: Death of a Dictator', ABC News, 2 April 1990.
2   Matthieu Ricard, *Altruism: The Power of Compassion to Change the World* (London: Atlantic Books, 2015).
3   'How to Let Altruism Be Your Guide', by Matthieu Ricard, TEDGlobal, 2014. https://www.ted.com /talks/matthieu_ricard_how_to_let_altruism _be_ your_guide?language=en

10. Welcome, Uncertainty

1   'Coroner slams delay over tinnitus sufferer who stabbed himself to death'. *The Telegraph*, 12 April 2012. www.telegraph.co.uk/news/health/news /9198029/Coroner-slams-delays-over-tinnitus -sufferer-who-stabbed-himself-to-death.html
2   Bhante Henepola Gunaratana, *Mindfulness in*

Plain English (Somerville, MA: Wisdom Publishing, 2002), p. 4.

11. Double Your Failure Rate

1 Alain de Botton, *The Consolations of Philosophy* (London: Hamish Hamilton, 2000), p. 206.
2 Ibid., p. 215.
3 Ibid.

12. On Ego and the Forces of Glamour

1 David Marcum and Steven Smith, *Egonomics: What makes ego our greatest asset (or most expensive liability)* (New York: Simon & Schuster, 2007).
2 Carl Jung, 'Spirit and Life' in *The Collected Works*, edited by Sir Herbert Read et al. (Princeton University Press, 1970).
3 Marianne Williamson, *A Return to Love* (New York: HarperCollins, 1992).
4 Martin Laird, *A Sunlit Absence* (Oxford: OUP, 2011).
5 Tim Ferriss, *The 4-Hour Body*, 'Closing Thoughts: The Trojan Horse' (New York: Harmony Books, 2010).

Acknowledgements

Thanks to the leaders, entrepreneurs, thought leaders and authors that have graciously shared their stories: Kaz Brecher, Katherine Collins, Chip Conley, Steve Damos, Uffe Elbæk, Jonathan Fields, James Flaherty, Betty Sue Flowers, R. Ed Freeman, Bo Heimann, Sky Shayne Innes, Claus Meyer, Peter Mellen, Kimbal Musk, Thea Polancic, Susan Salgado, John Sweeney, Kip Tindell, Ocean WhiteHawk and Marc Winn.

Several directors and faculty members at Ashridge Executive Education, a Hult International Business School, have been very generous with their time, ideas and research, including: Tanja D. Levine, Vicki Culpin, Megan Reitz, Chris Nichols, Mike Grandinetti, Trudi West and Jim Sintros.

Thank you also to our wonderful editors at Pan Macmillan, Robin Harvie, Zennor Compton, Laura Carr, Cindy Chan and Laura Langlois, and to Morgwn Rimel at The School of Life.

Photographic Credits

The authors and publisher would like to thank the following for permission to reproduce the images used in this book:

Page 11 First Lady Nancy Reagan applauding Leonard Skutnik © Dirck Halstead / The LIFE Images Collection / Getty Images

Page 15 Two-week-old Baby / 1966 © Mary Evans Picture Library / ROGER MAYNE

Page 37 South Africa, Cape Town, motorcyclist sitting on rock at the coast enjoying view © Westend61 / Westend61

Page 43 René Descartes (1596–1650), illustration from *Le Plutarque Francais* by E. Mennechet, published in Paris, 1835 (colour engraving), Jacquand, Claude (1804–78) (after) / Bibliothèque des Arts Décoratifs, Paris, France / Archives Charmet / Bridgeman Images

Page 57 Wildlife © Kevin Schafer / Contributor / Getty Images

Explore All of the "Maintenance Manuals for
the Mind" from the School of Life Library

How to Think More About Sex
Alain de Botton

ISBN 978-1-250-03065-8 / E-ISBN 978-1-250-03066-5
www.picadorusa.com/
howtothinkmoreaboutsex

How to Stay Sane
Philippa Perry

ISBN 978-1-250-03063-4 / E-ISBN 978-1-250-03064-1
www.picadorusa.com/
howtostaysane

How to Find Fulfilling Work
Roman Krznaric

ISBN 978-1-250-03069-6 / E-ISBN 978-1-250-03070-2
www.picadorusa.com/
howtofindfulfillingwork

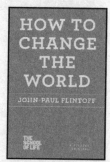

How to Change the World
John-Paul Flintoff

ISBN 978-1-250-03067-2 / E-ISBN 978-1-250-03068-9
www.picadorusa.com/
howtochangetheworld

PICADOR

www.picadorusa.com

Available wherever books and e-books are sold.

Explore All of the "Maintenance Manuals for the Mind" from the School of Life Library

How to Be Alone
Sara Maitland

ISBN 978-1-250-05902-4 / E-ISBN 978-1-250-05903-1
www.picadorusa.com/
howtobealone-maitland

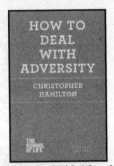

How to Deal with Adversity
Christopher Hamilton

ISBN 978-1-250-05900-0 / E-ISBN 978-1-250-05901-7
www.picadorusa.com/
howtodealwithadversity

How to Think About Exercise
Damon Young

ISBN 978-1-250-05904-8 / E-ISBN 978-1-250-05905-5
www.picadorusa.com/
howtothinkaboutexercise

How to Age
Anne Karpf

ISBN 978-1-250-05898-0 / E-ISBN 978-1-250-05899-7
www.picadorusa.com/
howtoage

PICADOR

www.picadorusa.com

Available wherever books and e-books are sold.